The Power Statement LOGBOOK

Mentoring the Habits of the Heart

A companion guide to the *Call of the Heart* series

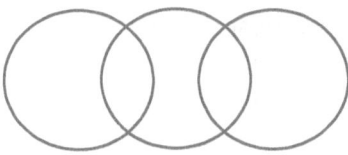

Empowering you to take charge of your journey.

Brian Roscoe

**THE POWER STATEMENT LOGBOOK:
MENTORING HABITS OF THE HEART**

COPYRIGHT © 2019 BY BRIAN ROSCOE

ALL RIGHTS RESERVED. NO PART OF THIS PUBLICATION MAY BE REPRODUCED, DISTRIBUTED, OR TRANSMITTED IN ANY FORM OR BY ANY MEANS, INCLUDING PHOTOCOPYING, RECORDING, OR OTHER ELECTRONIC OR MECHANICAL METHODS, WITHOUT THE PRIOR WRITTEN PERMISSION OF THE AUTHOR, EXCEPT IN THE CASE OF BRIEF QUOTATIONS EMBODIED IN CRITICAL REVIEWS AND CERTAIN OTHER NONCOMMERCIAL USES PERMITTED BY COPYRIGHT LAW.

THE CONTENT OF THIS BOOK IS FOR GENERAL INFORMATIONAL PURPOSES ONLY. IT IS NOT MEANT TO BE USED, NOR SHOULD IT BE USED, TO DIAGNOSE OR TREAT ANY MEDICAL CONDITION OR TO REPLACE THE SERVICES OF YOUR PHYSICIAN OR OTHER HEALTHCARE PROVIDER. THE ADVICE AND STRATEGIES CONTAINED IN THE BOOK MAY NOT BE SUITABLE FOR ALL READERS.

NEITHER THE AUTHOR, PUBLISHER, NOR ANY OF THEIR EMPLOYEES OR REPRESENTATIVES GUARANTEES THE ACCURACY OF INFORMATION IN THIS BOOK OR ITS USEFULNESS TO A PARTICULAR READER, NOR ARE THEY RESPONSIBLE FOR ANY DAMAGE OR NEGATIVE CONSEQUENCE THAT MAY RESULT FROM ANY TREATMENT, ACTION TAKEN, OR INACTION BY ANY PERSON READING OR FOLLOWING THE INFORMATION IN THIS BOOK.

FOR PERMISSION REQUESTS OR TO CONTACT THE AUTHOR, VISIT:
DRBRIANROSCOE.COM

ISBN-13: 978-0-9976476-7-9

PRINTED IN THE UNITED STATES OF AMERICA

The Power Statement LOGBOOK

Mentoring the habits of the heart

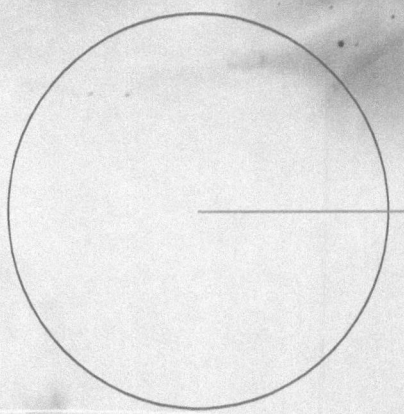

BRIAN ROSCOE
author of the Call of the Heart series

THANK YOU, THANK YOU,
I Cherish This

I think my job as a writer, and as a human dedicated to the knowledge of the heart, is to use my words to help others find ways to create more balance within. I want to inspire an opening up between wisdom, the essence of the heart, and the natural lean of the intellect—to build that internal bridge of connection between the mind and the heart that helps us transit our truest road of identity; a highway that runs from our head and unfolds into the master control room of our heart. This is where the work of life is done—the part of our journey that inspires us to grasp at and hold close the biggest picture of awareness and of our essence.

As I write, my goal is to take the concepts of the heart—the concepts of love, and wisdom, and personal expansion—and make them more accessible, more easy-going for the mind; to compassionately remember that our mind might have the tendency to see some of these lessons and growth as threatening or uncomfortable. So I try to describe the concepts of this journey to the heart in ways that won't jump deeply into complexity, but into a more easily integrated, understandable, and present form of finding power and wisdom within.

As our lives relate to Power Statements, we need to step back from the business of the mind and ask, *What are we saying to the universe as we explore it? What's our message when we find a phrase that really resonates with us, touches some part of us internally enough that we feel compelled to take note of it and write it down? What are we saying to the universe, our universe, when we find an exercise protocol, a meditation or a diet, or a particular way of being that allows us to expand into ourselves in a more tenacious, rewarding, and life-affirming way?* **We're** saying blatantly to our creation, "Thank you, thank you, I cherish this."

In essence, all these statements that we find our truth in are gratitude statements. They are thank you letters for life. We can only find them and see the truth in them when we're integrated with a state of appreciation for all that we've been gifted. We reach out and explore for clarity and tools for our journey when our questions become strong enough to inspire the courage of curiosity. We find our Power Statements for life as we're remembering our miracle, and as we're reclaiming the wisdom that we are, indeed, alive, strong, and infinite. This is the journey from the head to the heart. **Welcome.**

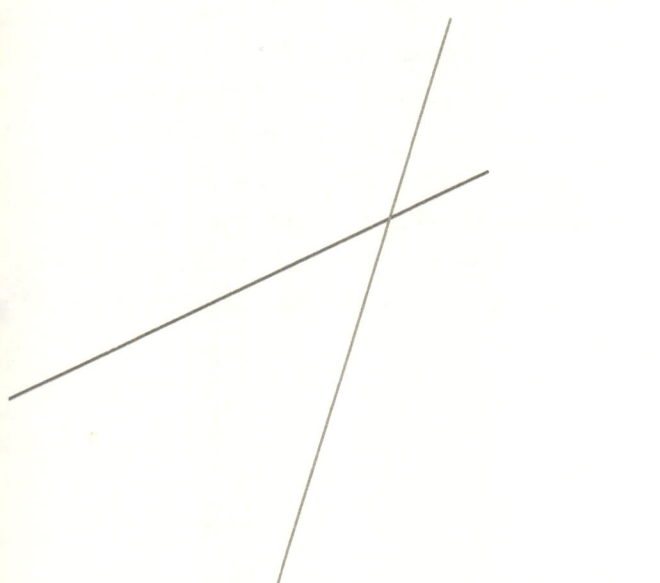

CONTENTS

Prolegomenon. i

Instructions. vii

PART ONE: Finding Words of Power
The Art of Finding Your Words. 1

PART TWO: Ideas of Power
Power Statement Antidotes. 45
Listening for Power Statements. 75

PART THREE: Living Life as a Power Statement
Build a Power Statement. 97
Your Tribe of Choice is a Power Statement. 119

In Conclusion. 135

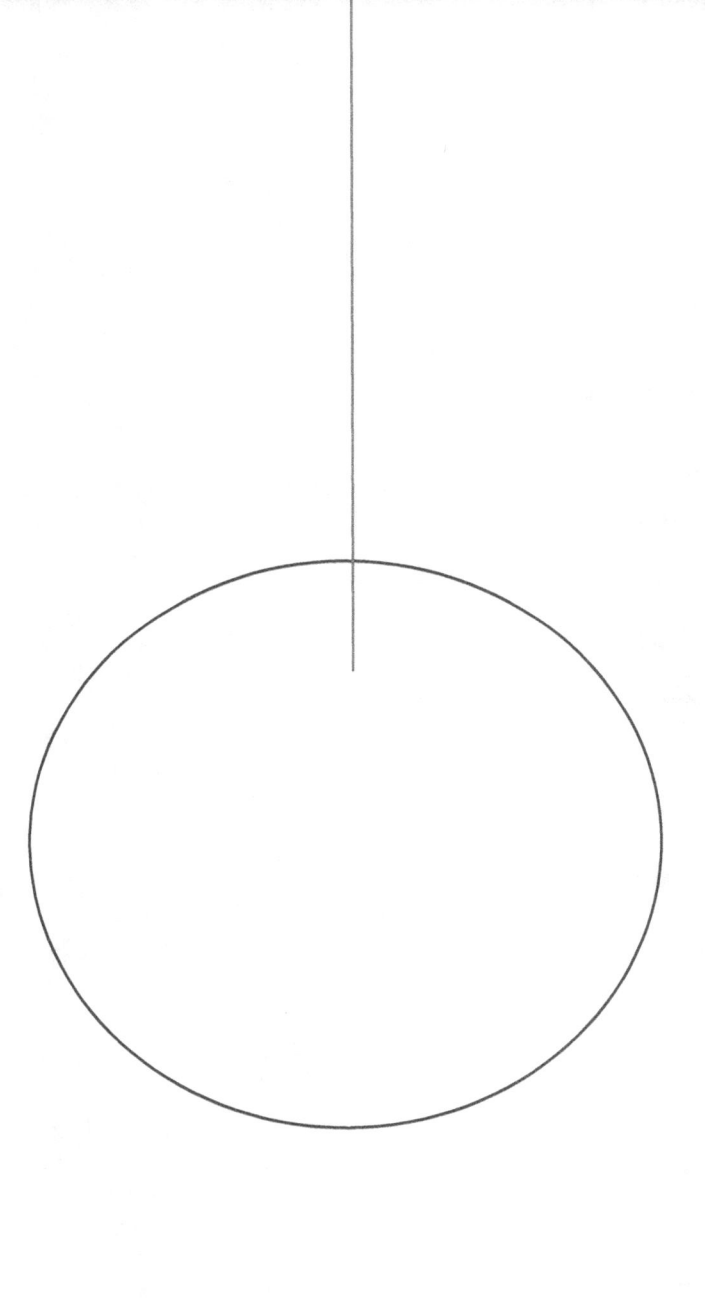

PROLEGOMENON

My hope for you is that you live your life as a gift; that you embrace the miracle of being alive, and immerse yourself in wisdom and strength, embracing all the lessons that life brings; that you seize what your heart so yearns for—love in all its many forms. I hope that you realize when you're stuck, struggling in negativity, wrestling with anxiety and in personal pain, that you can see that **your ability to thrive is limited only by the quality of your thinking.** Because our goal should always be to thrive in this life, to experience ourselves as one with its miracle, and to organize our world and ourselves in such a way that we allow life and all the expressions of love's presence to freely move through us.

Our human goal, no matter the words we use to portray it, is to *live, love, and thrive in a life of our own choosing.*

So choose your life with the strength and integrity of your inner warrior, and then welcome yourself—welcome yourself to your precious journey!

There are so many ways we can leverage ourselves in this journey, ways we can empower ourselves and our lives, to take full advantage of the precious time we have in this world. It's through claiming our courage and our love with integrity that we find the strength to journey forward into a life of reclaiming our own heart. Through our conviction to step into this world with all the forms of love, kindness, courage, and creativity, we offer ourselves and the world powerful statements of how we want to live. We offer affirmations of being alive in our words and actions that can inspire those around us as we lift ourselves toward an incredible life of our own choosing—a journey through the heart. It's here that we can remember ourselves with an authenticity that honors the life that flows through us.

We are, indeed, co-creators in this world we call home. And we're here to become the best of ourselves, to open our hearts and help create a life where we can walk with the strength and heart of the spirited warrior we are. Together, we can all help to shape this world. We have to choose to give ourselves to it, choose to bring our best. For the warrior, it's our destiny, our responsibility, and our duty to do so. And it takes heart, integrity, and strength. It requires your love and the best of you, and, make no mistake about it, it's work! So put on your boots and your overalls, because when you choose the path of the heart and the journey of the spiritual warrior, life changes and moves through you in ways you've probably not experienced before, and, boy, does it get busy!

So once again, *welcome to your beautiful journey.*

POWER STATEMENT LOGBOOK

Remember your heart,
learn to listen to it and follow its guidance,
use its wisdom to move through this precious life with a vitality
and a comfort so deep, so profound, that words will feel unnecessary.

"To know thyself is the beginning of wisdom."
–Socrates

ROSCOE

So Where the Heck Did I Write That Down?!

I think everyone finds quotes, ideas, and concepts of life that they resonate with—little golden nuggets of life and wisdom we want to be able to hold and refer back to periodically. And if you're like me, you collect these various quotes and lifestyle ideas from all kinds of different people, sources, and places. Quotes from authors, books, movies, cartoons, as well as scripture, conversation tidbits with friends, ideas from just listening to what's going on around you, TV, the internet, radio interview quotes, people chatting, lectures and sermons, and the list goes on. These are the thoughts and ideas that we feed off of. They're the reminders of life, the concepts that help you remember and cultivate who you are, who you're becoming now—the ideas that we move through the world with, that we aspire to become or return to in this life, in this human form. And we need learn to keep track of them.

Perhaps you have very special words that touch you beyond just the simplicity of that one word. It touches your heart in a far more expansive way, an ineffable way. These are the words that can hold a deeper meaning that surpass the intellect behind the word. Gratitude, forgiveness, compassion, caring, love, heart—the words that we live our inspired life through. All you need to do is whisper them and they create an opening, a feeling, and a remembering within. They remind you of who you are or, at the very least, what you're becoming.

That's what the *Power Statement Logbook* is all about: reminding you of the truths you hold and the wisdom that directs you. It's about helping you cultivate the ideas of the heart that you yearn for. The logbook provides a framework for you to help those concepts grow within you—it produces a way for you to grab ahold of that golden idea that came to you almost surreptitiously, but obviously in synchronicity with your path, your journey. The logbook allows you to move through life with all your Power Statements by your side, nurturing you, helping you build and remember your miracle.

So, here's to you!
Cheers to the Power Statements that feed your heart!
And *welcome to your journey.*

Power Statements = Claiming Your Life Presence in This World

Consider all the powerful ways you can make a statement about who you are. Look at what your life is driven by, and how you're motivated to live in this moment. Do you make your choices from a place of strength rather than fear? Do you create your life rather than having it created for you? Imagine who you become as you live life in the full abundance of who you are, exploring and being driven by your strength of heart.

Who is that person? That heart? What changes in your everyday walking world when you put on those easily forgotten shoes? Who do you become when you let yourself run in the wind, unfettered and unencumbered by the limitations of the mind, relying only on your heart for direction? If you never ask the question, expecting answers might prove rather fruitless.

The Power Statements we hold can come as words or actions. They can be seen in the things we do for others, how we treat ourselves, or in what we do because we simply know it's right. Because it's through our Power Statements that we reflect our inner selves out into the world—we reflect the quality of life we hold within our heart.

> "Take chances, make mistakes. That's how you grow. Pain nourishes your courage. You have to fail in order to practice being brave."
> –Mary Tyler Moore

INSTRUCTIONS

In the *Power Statement Logbook*, you'll find sections that present some curious ideas to look at regarding our interaction with this world—a world that often seems to be teeming with pure motivation. And there are also little inspirational paragraphs at the beginning of some sections, just trying to fire you up for a little self-exploration. These are fire starters, my attempts at creating motivation for your warrior. My suggestion is to let life move through you and give your inner fire permission to ignite. Life seems far more about going out and finding your own Power Statements than following someone else's; it's about exploring and paying attention to what unfolds for you, in you, through you, what ends up serendipitously in your lap. That's why we're asking questions and leaving space for answers and research—for you to chronicle your own precious, unique, wonderful, and powerful heart. *This book is meant to help you light that match.*

The point of having a logbook:

The *Power Statement Logbook* is a way of giving to yourself, giving your body, your mind and soul, permission to show up to life with the greatest potential and integrity. **Make no mistake about it: this is a workbook. It's meant to exploit your heart, to entice your journey, and to expand your life.**

When we find something that has meaning to us—anything that simultaneously tickles our mind and ignites our soul—the logbook gives us the permission and a place to pause for a moment, and a space to write that treasure down. The *Power Statement Logbook* is your mechanism to log in and have a handy way to retrieve that point of information that spiked your attention. It's something we need, because remembering all the quotes and concepts that we come across during a busy week can be daunting, even stressful, when we try and hold it all in our heads. And it's just unproductive to being present. The truth of it is, we're not meant to walk around with all that chatter in our minds. We just want to be able to hold and have the opportunity to refer back to the essence of things we see as important when we have time; to reconnect with the feeling of that wisdom nugget or that inspired idea for life.

So, please, freely write in this book. It's designed for your scribbles and comments. It's meant to put notes in, to remind you how to find the statements, websites, authors, books, movies, articles, people, places, and things that turn you on!

As far as the *Power Statement Logbook* is concerned, you have complete permission to do whatever you need to do with it in order to facilitate your journey. Do whatever you want, wherever you need—turn the corners on pages, rip, tear, slash, scribble, blot out what doesn't work. You can do anything you want, because it's all for the sake of your journey. You're trying to create something for yourself here, so dispense with any judgment or book rules, or etiquette you might have and make this your book! Jump in! After all, you're worth it!

Choosing Qualities of Thought, Creating Qualities of Life

In life, we all have moments where we realize that we're out of sorts and we need to, in some way, reclaim ourselves, to reconnect with life and pull our hearts back into the game. We see that we've lost track of our journey, and we need to again explore what's meaningful—decide how we want to live. See this book as an exercise in recognizing, defining, and holding your truth. Allow it to be a framework of rediscovering yourself, to know that deeper love within, to develop a stronger sense of character and healthy personal power, and to redefine yourself through a presence of heart.

We're all responsible in a very individual way for claiming our power. That power is a force connected through our free will choice, and is the primary influence we use in choosing how we see our life and how we intend to live it. It drives our conscious thought, which, in turn, drives the journey of how we live. We're choosing an internal stance that proclaims, "I am strong. I am alive and awake. And I am worth it. This is who I am."

Choosing your Power Statements is a journey in choosing the quality of your world. It's your personal contribution to how you will experience life. Your Power Statements help you decide the tone and emotional flow of your life, and they represent the choice of thinking that you define your days with. As we claim a life that points us toward our truth, we're naturally invited into a deep and personal experience of our own authenticity. And in that, we learn that we are worthy of a life in which

the full presence of love is available to us in all its forms. Ultimately, the *Power Statement Logbook* is designed to help you connect with that love, and help you reflect it into your unique and precious life. Can we really ask for anything more profound than that?

Making Statements of Intention Through Power Statements: I Am Engaged!

Our Power Statements put our intention to communicate to the universe into action, to say, "We're engaged with exploring and living through our wild truth!" We're telling our world we're in that we're on target with being alive to our journey! That we're open to find, utilize, and cultivate whatever tools we can to keep us integrated and focused on our target! **We know our job: staying centered on truth and always looking toward and into our heart.**

Part One
Finding Words of Power

The Art of Finding YOUR WORDS
Finding Your infinite Power

The Infinite Power Statements Moving Through Words

Yes, words. Both singular in their form and use, as well as together in their infinite combinations. Words are the stuff that Power Statements come alive through! Vitally important to our world, our evolution, and our growth, words are deeply inspired gifts to us. Depending on the version, even in the Bible it says something like, "In the beginning was the Word, and the Word was with God, and the Word was God." Well, that's quite the statement, and proof enough for me that words hold power. There's got to be a reason behind a statement like that.

Think about it. It's through this miracle of words that we express ourselves, through words that we try to expand our understanding of creation. It's words that help us move our thoughts into the world, words that help us create a profound ability to communicate with one another, and it's through our words that we build pictures in our own minds and

in the minds of others that inspire a deep connection with being alive. Now isn't that all part of being connected to this miracle of words?

I've always felt that it's truly miraculous that we're able to connect to and interact with one another through a language of words. The complexity of it all really shocks me—the ability to push air through our windpipes and come up with sounds that have so much meaning and potential behind them, not to mention all the gestures and body movements suggesting words and depicting communication. Language is an amazing, precious gift of our human experience, to be valued and not to be taken for granted. What we do with our words can be spectacular, or, if we choose, can cause horrendous pain. Our words are not to be trifled with. They're to be honored and used with respect, and one of the many ways we can do this is with our Power Statements.

Look for your Power Statements through any avenue of communication available: simple words, simple phrases, quotes, songs, magazines, books, poems, prayers, meditations. And do it through whatever reliable source or medium you want. What's important is that you look, and that what you find has heart.

Pay attention to the more ineffable Power Statements of simply being present—the power found in the new-now. These practices may not require our spoken words, but they will naturally inspire them. Consider things like meditation, prayer, or even the simple quiet while sitting in the woods or during a sunset. As you participate in these, before, during, and afterward, pay attention to the words that naturally come forward, let yourself be surprised by the quotes and poems you synchronistically find, and the ideas that seem to spontaneously present themselves. This is your listening heart at work, lining up your life so that what you need to grow is always given the opportunity to be noticed. **So be sure to take a note!**

And let the limit of your Power Statement subject only be limited by your infinite imagination. Pay attention to the statements that are cultivated through taking care of yourself, to Power Statements on the power of intention, personal volition, expressions of love, and self-love, to Power Statements held in our actions, doing and caring for yourself, doing for others, the intention held in life, the Power Statements of self-care: exercise, meditation, healthcare, diet, creating healthy relationships, learning strong communication. All these Power Statement will naturally evolve into a language of description and movement through you. Remember them, and, again, take a note so you can remember them and build on their strength.

Open up to and explore what's already in your environment:
- What movies, literature, music, podcasts, or programming do you already have, listen to, and love because of the messages they have?
- Write down what strikes you. Grab any kind of book, especially one like *Inspirational Espresso*, as you flip through magazines, comic books, health flyers, newspapers. You can find a ton of inspiring and growth-oriented ideas to draw from just floating around. These publications are meant to inspire the mind in some direction. It's up to you where you go with it.

- Talking with friends is an awesome source of inspiration and wisdom. Ask them what they're drawn to, who they admire, what they're inspired by, and where their greatest growth comes from. They might not have an answer right away, and think you're a little weird, but they likely already knew that, and that's probably why they love you. But questions like these are the ones people walk away with and think about, and they tend to encourage conversations later.

- Pay attention to the phrases that strike you when you're watching a movie, listening to the radio or a podcast. Again, someone has put some real thought into these productions, they're meant to catch your attention.

- And, of course, the internet is flooded with inspirational sayings, not to mention its share of negativity. So search smart, look for your concepts of mindfulness, wisdom, exercises and techniques of health, meditation, and heart-centered inspiration. Explore and find your tools

- As far as the negativity, wish them peace and let it show you what you don't want to involve yourself with. That's a huge lesson within itself.

EXPLORING

What ideas in this abundant world tugs on the strings of your heart? What speaks to you? What drives you to act?

What concepts of living, ideas of the spirit, interests of the mind and intellect are you drawn to in this abundant world? Where does your heart consistently and stubbornly point you, and what does it draw you into despite the temptations of a distracting and often misleading mind? How does your heart try to pull you from the shell you've surrounded yourself with, and away from all the dogma held in your human opinions? Can you hear the whispering heart as it attempts to influence the soul of your life?

This is where you look for your Power Statements. It's in this place, within the core of who you are, that you authentically present yourself to yourself, and open to the world, paving your own road to re-discover yourself. This is you giving your pure light to what's happening inside of and through you.

Explore and nurture your heart. Open to what's moving through you, open to the wisdom and truth that asks for expression. Pay attention to the internal communication that takes place beyond the mouth, and give language to the light of being alive.

What are you drawn to? How do you best learn and absorb? By reading, hearing the spoken word, visually, watching an example? It's likely your go-to mode of exploring the world. So pay attention to that. Use it, but don't neglect the other avenues of exploration, because there's huge value in those approaches, too.

- What concepts draw you in?
- What ideas touch you?
- What surprises you about this life?
- What ideas are you scared to explore, but curious to understand?
- Who were you before you were born to this world?
- Ask questions about things that shock you. The secrets. The non-conforming ideas in the world.
- What uniqueness in this abundant world calls for your exploration?
- What uniqueness do you bring to this world—a wonder already held within you?

Explore and stay open to all your questions of life, your desires for knowledge, all your curiosities, and confusion. Explore all the movements in your mind and take note, and then explore for the answers, and learn what feeds your heart.

Category Suggestions

These are suggestions of where I tend to find my words and statements. They're categories based on my experiences, what I've noticed brings me inspiration through the day, the stuff that I'm paying attention to. They fall into some basic categories: words, phrases, concepts and ideas that strike me, often quite coincidentally, depending on what's going on in my life. When I'm working on something, clarifying some concept, inevitably, help on some level pops up in the form of a concept or idea, and I try it on. If it fits, I include it in my life.

These can become the things I don't want to forget about, the words and concepts I come across that have inspired me, that have made me question whether I want to move away from or towards them.

Categories may include any and all of the written or spoken word:

- **Individual words of power:** *i.e.: some personal favorites are "ineffable," "gratitude," "courage"*
- **Various quotes from anywhere:** *t-shirts are a personal favorite.*
- **Quotes from books**
- **Quotes from websites**
- **Quotes from all the various sharing social networks**
- **Quotes from movies:** *i.e.: "Simba, you are more than you have become." -The Lion King*
- **Words from friends that care, and those that drive you nuts**
- **Happenstance words from strangers:** you just happened to be in the right place at the right time
- **Quotes from the radio, TV shows, podcasts, YouTube talks, lectures of all kinds:** *i.e.: talk radio works well for this, interviews and educational discussion. I like shows like On Being or some of the BBC and NPR specials.*

We naturally find inspiration and connection in life when we're paying attention; the wisdom found in our synchronistic moments: Quotes and words of power found through any of our community relations *(I've included some examples of my own little moments)*:

- **Friendships**
- **Employment:** *i.e.: an old boss of mine once said, "Every job takes three months before you even begin to feel comfortable with it; at LEAST three months." This has helped me through the years with all kinds of new endeavors.*
- **Education**
- **Diet advice:** *i.e.: "Try and eat colorfully."*
- **Exercise advice:** *i.e.: "Do your best and forget the rest!" -Tony Horton. This can influence our approach to many aspects of our lives.*
- **Prayer**
- **Meditation:** *i.e.: "Touch your heart and take a breath."*
- **Leisure time**
- **Exploring personal interests**
- **Exploring passions:** *i.e.: I always define my main passion in life as reconnecting with the essence of my heart, so common power words for me are: "reclaiming," "reclaiming self," "remembering," or, "remembering essence"*
- **The gold synchronistically found as soon as you choose to open to what your journey is offering you**

POWER STATEMENT LOGBOOK

Feel free to use this as a labeling system to help keep track of all the possible categories that can help establish strength, productivity, and spirit in this journey. Life gives us so much to draw from, feel free to insert your own categories. This world is abundant with intentional and unintentional reminders for the heart, constantly trying to point us towards who we are. Take advantage of them, explore your destiny!

- **Internet:**
- **Books:**
- **Authors:**
- **Speakers:**
- **Friends:**
- **Heroes:**

- **Leaders:**
- **Magazines:**
- **Movies:**
-
-
-

Words Express Energy

Words are energy. Period. They produce internal experiences for us, delivering the power to hurt and to heal. Words open us up to the miracle of communication, and they rock our world every day, in all kinds of ways. Words are powerful. Use them as an extension of yourself, to project your truth and to expand your heart. Use your miracle language with honor and respect. Use it to help, not hinder, and use it to expand life, not suppress it. Words have energy.

We put a lot of effort into life, investigating our human experience in all its forms. Words are a huge part of it. We're all busy exploring our communication, various forms of literature and media, quotes, words, interactions of all kinds, and the human meaning behind all these words is a wonderful exercise for the heart. Participating in life with our words, whether written, spoken, signed, read or listened to, is like saying thank you to the universe, thank you to God, thank you for the gift of being alive, the privilege of being human. What an adventure!

These are some words to draw inspiration from:

Finding what's important to you, what speaks to you, what inspires your heart, is not always easy. Sometimes, it requires a little exploration. Below is a list of potential words that might whisper to you. Find the ones that touch deepest within, the words and concepts that call for your attention, or even the ones that create resistance in you. Pay attention to what inspires joy, pain, laughter, or tears, because it's in that pop of emotion that you see what needs to be worked on and explored within.

POWER STATEMENT LOGBOOK

Words That Ask You to Think!

The list below is to assist you in exploring categories of interest and subjects to research and consider. Complete the missing synonyms and antonyms, exploring the function of each word. Each word carries its own energy.

A

Abundance
Synonyms: *bountiful, thriving, wealth*
Antonyms: *lack*

Adaptability
Synonyms:
Antonyms:

Acceptance
Synonyms:
Antonyms:

Action
Synonyms:
Antonyms:

Alive
Synonyms: *living your dreams, living your life, living Spirit*
Antonyms:

Alternatives
Synonyms:
Antonyms:

Appreciation:
Synonyms: *gratitude, thanks, admiration, regard*
Antonyms: *criticism, disparagement*

Awareness:
Synonyms: *consciousness, experience, realization, recognition, understanding, enlightenment, mindfulness, presence, sentience*
Antonyms: *unconsciousness, ignorance, neglect*

B

Balance
Synonyms:
Antonyms:

Beginning
Synonyms:
Antonyms:

Beginning Again
Synonyms: *starting over, fresh start, giving yourself permission to begin again*
Antonyms:

Believing in Yourself
Synonyms: *self love, courage*
Antonyms:

Beauty
Synonyms:
Antonyms:

Becoming
Synonyms: *transformation*
Antonyms:

Becoming Whole
Synonyms: *healing*
Antonyms:

Blessings
Synonyms:
Antonyms:

Boundaries
Synonyms: *respecting boundaries, healthy boundaries*
Antonyms:

Breath
Synonyms: *breathing, breath of life, prana, considered as a life-giving force, Prāṇāyāma*
Antonyms:

C

Caring
Synonyms:
Antonyms:

Centered
Synonyms:
Antonyms:

Challenge
Synonyms:
Antonyms:

Change
Synonyms:
Antonyms:

Cherish
Synonyms:
Antonyms:

Clarity
Synonyms:
Antonyms:

Courage
Synonyms: *brave*
Antonyms:

> *If courage is a quality that inspires you, consider exploring quotes from people like Maya Angelou or Winston Churchill.*
>
> *"Courage is what it takes to stand up and speak; courage is also what it takes to sit down and listen."*
> -Winston Churchill
>
> *"Still, like air, I rise."*
> -Maya Angelou

Confidence
Synonyms:
Antonyms:

Companionship
Synonyms:
Antonyms:

Compassion
Synonyms:
Antonyms:

Communication
Synonyms:
Antonyms:

Contribution
Synonyms: *contributing to life*
Antonyms:

Calm
Synonyms: *peace*
Antonyms:

Commitment
Synonyms:
Antonyms:

Consciousness
Synonyms:
Antonyms:

Creativity
Synonyms:
Antonyms:

Claim
Synonyms: *as in to claim your life, claim your peace, reclaim yourself*
Antonyms:

Cultivate
Synonyms: *growing, creating, enriching, as in a deeper awareness of yourself, or cultivating peace*
Antonyms:

Curiosity
Synonyms:
Antonyms:

D
Discernment
Synonyms:
Antonyms:

Divine
Synonyms: *divine connection, divine essence, divine love*
Antonyms:

Dedication
Synonyms: *drive, volition, integrity, devotion*
Antonyms:

Doing Your Best
Synonyms:
Antonyms:

E
Enlightenment
Synonyms:
Antonyms:

Engagement
Synonyms:
Antonyms:

Equality
Synonyms:
Antonyms:

Equanimity
Synonyms:
Antonyms:

Excellence
Synonyms:
Antonyms:

Expansiveness
Synonyms:
Antonyms:

Emotional Health
Synonyms:
Antonyms:

Encouragement
Synonyms:
Antonyms:

Essence
Synonyms: *true nature, essential essence, essence awareness*
Antonyms:

Education
Synonyms: *lessons, learning, exploring consciousness, life lessons*
Antonyms:

Emergence
Synonyms:
Antonyms:

Encouragement
Synonyms:
Antonyms:

Enthusiasm
Synonyms: *excitement, zeal*
Antonyms:

Energy
Synonyms: *mojo*
Antonyms:

F

Faith
Synonyms:
Antonyms:

Forgiveness
Synonyms:
Antonyms:

Family
Synonyms: *tribe, community, friends, soulmates, team, teamwork*
Antonyms:

Flexibility
Synonyms:
Antonyms:

Free-Spirited
Synonyms: *truth, true nature, authenticity, free-thinking*
Antonyms:

Freedom
Synonyms: *liberation*
Antonyms:

Free Will
Synonyms:
Antonyms:

G

Generosity
Synonyms: *giving, passing it forward, sharing*
Antonyms:

Gift
Synonyms:
Antonyms:

Grateful
Synonyms:
Antonyms:

Gratitude
Synonyms:
Antonyms:

Graciousness
Synonyms:
Antonyms:

Greeting
Synonyms:
Antonyms:

Gentleness
Synonyms: *Ease*
Antonyms:

Goal
Synonyms:
Antonyms:

Grit
Synonyms: *strength, courage, tenacity, stick-to-it-ness*
Antonyms:

Grace
Synonyms:
Antonyms:

Growth
Synonyms: *grow*
Antonyms:

Guidance
Synonyms:
Antonyms:

Going Within
Synonyms:
Antonyms:

Goodness
Synonyms:
Antonyms:

Group Mind
Synonyms:
Antonyms:

H

Harmony
Synonyms:
Antonyms:

Health
Synonyms: *body health, mind health, spirit health, mental health, planetary health, true health*
Antonyms:

Higher Good
Synonyms:
Antonyms:

 ROSCOE

Honor
Synonyms:
Antonyms:

Home
Synonyms:
Antonyms:

Hope
Synonyms:
Antonyms:

Honesty
Synonyms:
Antonyms:

Humility
Synonyms:
Antonyms:

Happy
Synonyms:
Antonyms:

Heart
Synonyms: *heart space, heartfelt*
Antonyms:

Heart-Centered
Synonyms: *all heart, heart-centered choices*
Antonyms:

Humility
Synonyms:
Antonyms: *Hubris*

I

Imagination
Synonyms:
Antonyms:

Innocence
Synonyms:
Antonyms:

Infinity
Synonyms:
Antonyms:

Integrity
Synonyms: *the ability to say yes or no with wisdom*
Antonyms:

Internal Awareness
Synonyms: *internal dialogue, internal stance, internal talk, internal growth, knowing yourself*
Antonyms:

Inspiration
Synonyms:
Antonyms:

Insight
Synonyms: *inspired ideas*
Antonyms:

Instincts
Synonyms:
Antonyms:

Interdependence
Synonyms: *higher union*
Antonyms:

Intuition
Synonyms: *foresight, knowing*
Antonyms:

Introspection
Synonyms:
Antonyms:

J

Journey
Synonyms: *paths*
Antonyms:

Joy
Synonyms: *joyful*
Antonyms:

Justice
Synonyms: *just, honorable, strength, loving strength*
Antonyms:

K

Kindness
Synonyms:
Antonyms:

Knowledge
Synonyms:
Antonyms:

L

Laughter
Synonyms:
Antonyms:

Leadership
Synonyms:
Antonyms:

Life Lessons
Synonyms: *education, learning, exploring, as in expanding consciousness*
Antonyms:

Life
Synonyms: *life energy, life-giving, light, our light*
Antonyms:

Listening
Synonyms:
Antonyms:

Living Deliberately
Synonyms: *tenacity, volition, independence, "independent of the good opinions of others," living your own life, be the example, spreading your wings, stand on your own, stepping up to the plate, standing strong*
Antonyms: *self-imprisonment, restricted, self-restricted, self-limiting*

Loyal
Synonyms:
Antonyms:

Letting Go
Synonyms: *release, releasing*
Antonyms:

Living as an Example
Synonyms: *being the example*
Antonyms:

Love, Unconditional Love, Loving One Another, Self-Love, Planetary Love
Synonyms:
Antonyms:

M

Making a Difference
Synonyms:
Antonyms:

Magical
Synonyms:
Antonyms:

Motivation
Synonyms:
Antonyms:

Mind-Body
Synonyms:
Antonyms:

Mindfulness
Synonyms:
Antonyms:

Miracles
Synonyms: *miraculous*
Antonyms:

Moderation
Synonyms:
Antonyms:

Movement
Synonyms: *mobility*
Antonyms:

Mystical
Synonyms: *mystery*
Antonyms:

N

Next Step
Synonyms: *forward movement*
Antonyms:

Noble
Synonyms: *wisdom*
Antonyms:

Non-Material
Synonyms: *ineffable*
Antonyms:

Not Personalizing
Synonyms: *not taking events personal*
Antonyms:

Nurturing
Synonyms:
Antonyms:

O

Overcoming Adversity
Synonyms: *rising above*
Antonyms:

Optimism
Synonyms:
Antonyms:

Opportunity
Synonyms:
Antonyms:

Open
Synonyms: *opening, open-mindedness, opening up*
Antonyms:

P

Parenting
Synonyms: *mentoring, teacher, sage*
Antonyms:

Passion
Synonyms:
Antonyms:

Patience
Synonyms:
Antonyms:

Peace, Peace of Mind
Synonyms:
Antonyms:

Play
Synonyms: *laugh, gregarious*
Antonyms:

Power
Synonyms:
Antonyms:

Practice
Synonyms:
Antonyms:

Purpose
Synonyms:
Antonyms:

Presence
Synonyms:
Antonyms:

Precious
Synonyms:
Antonyms:

Perseverance
Synonyms: *prevail, persistence*
Antonyms:

Pioneering
Synonyms: *pathfinder, entrepreneur*
Antonyms:

Potential
Synonyms:
Antonyms:

Perception
Synonyms:
Antonyms:

Q

Quality of Thought
Synonyms: *integrity of thought*
Antonyms:

 ROSCOE

Quiet
Synonyms: *quiet time, silence, solitude, peacefulness, settling, stilling your thoughts*
Antonyms:

R

Recharge
Synonyms: *charge your inner battery, rejuvenate, reset, reconnect*
Antonyms:

Reevaluation
Synonyms: *refine*
Antonyms:

Remembering
Synonyms: *remembering truth, resurfacing*
Antonyms:

Resiliency
Synonyms:
Antonyms:

Respect
Synonyms: *reverence*
Antonyms:

Relaxation
Synonyms: *rest, heal*
Antonyms:

Rebirth
Synonyms:
Antonyms:

S

Sacred
Synonyms: *sacredness, sacred journey, sacred path, sacred space*
Antonyms:

Sacrifice
Synonyms:
Antonyms:

Safe
Synonyms: *safety, belonging, secure*
Antonyms:

Sanctuary
Synonyms:
Antonyms:

Self, Self-Love, Self-Regulation, Self-Care, Self-Evolvement, Self-Knowledge, Self-Reliant, Self-Sufficient, Self-Respect
Synonyms:
Antonyms:

Spiritual, Physical, and Emotional Flexibility
Synonyms:
Antonyms:

Sensitivity
Synonyms:
Antonyms:

Service
Synonyms:
Antonyms:

Signs
Synonyms:
Antonyms:

Sight
Synonyms:
Antonyms:

Smile
Synonyms:
Antonyms:

Soul
Synonyms:
Antonyms:

Spirit
Synonyms:
Antonyms:

Steadfast
Synonyms:
Antonyms:

Stewardship
Synonyms:
Antonyms:

Strength
Synonyms:
Antonyms:

Singing
Synonyms:
Antonyms:

Stamina
Synonyms:
Antonyms:

Sweetness of Life
Synonyms:
Antonyms:

T

Talent
Synonyms:
Antonyms:

Thought
Synonyms:
Antonyms:

Trust
Synonyms:
Antonyms:

Tolerance
Synonyms:
Antonyms:

U

Underlying Purpose
Synonyms: *basic, elemental purpose*
Antonyms: *secondary, distraction*

Understanding
Synonyms: *integrity, harmony, agreement*
Antonyms: *confusion, discord*

Unity
Synonyms: *peace, solidarity, harmony*
Antonyms: *disagreement, discord*

V

Vision
Synonyms: *perception, acumen*
Antonyms: *sightlessness*

Vibrant
Synonyms: *vitality, active, dynamic*
Antonyms: *apathetic, lethargic, dispirited*

Value
Synonyms: *adore, admire, applaud*
Antonyms: *detractors, detriment*

W

Warrior
Synonyms: *champion, fighter, hero*
Antonyms:

Wellbeing, Wellbeing of the Body, Wellbeing of the Mind, Wellbeing of the Spirit, Wellbeing of the Soul
Synonyms: *comfort, contentment, health*
Antonyms: *danger, injury*

Wholeness
Synonyms: *entirety, integrity*
Antonyms: *incompleteness, partialness*

Wisdom
Synonyms: *experience, insight, acumen*
Antonyms: *ignorance, insensitivity*

Wonder
Synonyms: *amazement, Astonishment, Awe*
Antonyms:

Welcome, as in a Welcoming Posture in Life, Welcoming Change, Welcoming Life, Welcoming Love, Welcoming the Journey
Synonyms: *appreciated, desirable, gratifying*
Antonyms: *unacceptable*

POWER STATEMENT LOGBOOK

"Surely, life is not merely a job, an occupation; life is something extraordinarily wide and profound, it is a great mystery, a vast realm in which we function as human beings."
– Jiddu Krishnamurti

Exploring Words From Other Languages

Exploring words can be fun! No, really. It can be, especially words from different cultures and languages. If you want to spice up the journey of being human a bit, consider exploring words from other languages. All languages have their limitations, and English is no exception. It certainly has its drawbacks when it comes to finding precise words that express complex emotions and the concepts surroudning being human. Other languages and cultures have words for our human experience that English may not have developed. These other languages have explored and developed words for feelings and our connection with spirit and heart that are uniquely authentic to them, and worthy of our curious examination.

So often the meaning behind a word draws a picture in your mind that creates a feeling you just want to hold and remember—to nurture the concept within yourself and make it part of your world. So if it's in you, go ahead and explore the words and phrases invented by different languages, tribes, and cultures. You'll find that we all think about the same stuff, it's just that different groups develop more expressive words around different experiences. Explore, see how others see and describe our common human adventure—*life*.

Following is a list of words from a variety of cultures, words from around the world with no exact English equivalent. Each one is accompanied by a small discussion explaining their origin, the intent, and the meaning of the word. Some are quite thought-provoking and inspiring, they might even motivate you to explore a little further on your own.

Personally, I love the creative differences of cultural greetings. They're all so unique in their intention and message. I am always intrigued at how we see one another. So that's what I'm going to start with!

So many cultures around the world regard greeting one another as something far more than just a pleasantry, a simple hello, how-are-ya passing platitude. Greeting happens from the heart and soul of who we are. It opens us to the opportunities of simply touching and being touched by one another with a grace and honor. A gift deserved by all.

Sawubona (Zulu)
The Zulu greeting "sawubona" means "we see you." They use "we" instead of "I" because they believe that their eyes are connected to their ancestors' eyes. The other person would respond with "ngikhona," which means "I am here," or "yabo, sawubona," meaning "yes, we see you, too." By letting them know that you see them, you are inviting them to participate in your life with deep witnessing.

Zdraveite (Bulgarian)
This word is derived from the Bulgarian word "zdrave," which means "health." When people say hello in Bulgaria, they are wishing the other person to stay safe and healthy.

Aloha (Hawaiian)
According to a folk etymology, the word "aloha" is a compound of the Hawaiian word "alo," meaning "presence," "face," and "share," and "ha," meaning "essence of life." It is a greeting said from the heart with feelings of mutual regard and affection, love, peace, and compassion, with no obligation to receive anything in return.

Shalom (Hebrew)

"Shalom alechem" is a Hebrew greeting meaning "peace be upon you." The response being "alechem shalom" or "unto you, peace." This form of greeting is traditional among Jews throughout the world. The plural form is used even when addressing one person because one greets both the body and the soul. "Shalom" also connotes completeness, wholeness, health, peace, welfare, safety, soundness, tranquility, prosperity, perfectness, fullness, rest, harmony, and the absence of agitation or discord. When you say "shalom," you are wishing someone a wonderful life with everything that shalom represents!

Namasté (nah-mah-stay) (Hindu)

In the West, it's often heard at the end of yoga classes, and as we dig deeper into the intention and meaning behind it, we see that "namasté" is a salutation of respect and reverence. It literally translates to "I bow to you," however, in traditional Hinduism, it means "I bow to the divine in you" or, "the divine in me bows to the divine in you." "Namaste" can be spoken with or without the prayerful gesture of bringing ones palms together in front of the body (the palms and all ten fingers touch one another, with the thumbs joining in front of the heart space or brow) and gently bowing while speaking the greeting/blessing.

Hongi (Māori)

The traditional Māori greeting is called "the hongi." It's a greeting performed between two people by pressing their noses and often their foreheads together as they share a breath. In the hongi, the "ha" (breath of life) is exchanged in a symbolic show of unity. The greeting and exchange of breath can also be followed by a handshake. With this exchange, one is no longer considered simply a visitor, rather one of the people of the land.

Wabi Sabi (Japanese)

This term refers to finding the beauty in the imperfections of life and accepting that everything is constantly changing. The idea of wabi sabi comes from Buddhist teachings on impermanence, suffering, and emptiness or absence of self-nature.

In Japan, the concept of wabi sabi is seen as a universal view of life, centered on the acceptance of its inherent transience and imperfection. It describes an essence of beauty in life that is imperfect, impermanent, and incomplete. There's a rustic quality to objects described with the phrase "wabi sabi." A roughness, asymmetrical look, simple in nature and natural in appearance.

Modern use of the term connotes rustic simplicity, freshness or quietness, adding a uniqueness and elegance to the a beauty of an object, often seen as a serenity that comes with age. It can be applied to both natural and human-made objects, or understated elegance.

Firgun and Mudita

"Firgun" is a hebrew word, very similar to the concept of "mudita" (Sanskrit and Pali). They both denote the feeling of sympathetic or unselfish joy, or joy in the good fortune or success of others with a good heart and without jealousy. Jealousy and envy, as well as the German phrase "Schadenfreude" (when you take joy in someone else's misfortune), would be considered the opposite of "firgun" and "mudita."

Hygge (HEW-gə or HOO-ga) (both Danish and Norwegian)
Hygge is a warm, cozy feeling that washes over you; it needs to be experienced to be known. It's considered a quality of cosiness and good-natured warmth that inspires a feeling of contentment or wellbeing. The Danish consider it a defining characteristic of their culture.

It's a little confusing, but, in short, Hygge may originate from the word "hug," taken from an old Danish word meaning "to give courage, comfort, joy." In Old Norse, the word "hugr" later becames "hug," and means the soul, mind, and consciousness.

So then, can it be that a hug is an embrace of the soul, mind, and consciousness that's meant to help us bring courage, comfort, and joy to one another?

Meraki, (mer-a-ki) (modern Greek)
Meraki means doing something with a deep sense of spirit. It's used to describe what happens when you leave a piece of yourself (your soul, creativity, or love) in your work. When you love doing anything so much that you put "something of yourself" into what you're doing, it's a true labor of love. *Hmmm, sounds like writing to me… What a great title!* And am I stretching too far by thinking that it kind of sounds like the word "miracle?"

Nunchi (Korean)
"Nunchi" literally translates as "eye measure." It's having the ability to determine others' moods, resulting in knowing what to say or not to say or do in a given situation simply by being in their presence and/or

listening to them. Nunchi is having the ability to communicate through body language, gestures and intuition, it's the subtle art of listening on a higher level to others and being able to gauge their state of wellbeing as you relate to them. In Korea, people can be considered as having different qualities of nunchi: a high level of or an absence of nunchi, or even quick witted nunchi, are typical observations. In the West, this might be seen as having a particular level of emotional intelligence, or even as being empathic.

Strikhedonia (Greek)
This is the pleasure of being able to say, "To hell with it!" I actually love this word, not as an active aggression or bad feeling toward anything, but as an act of freeing oneself from old thinking that needs to be let go of.

Talk about being in the joy of finally being able to let go of something we may have held as a burden for a very long time. How wonderful and empowering it is to the heart when we can do it without resentment or taking it personally.

Gunnen (Dutch)
Similar to "firgun" and "mudita," "gunnen" is the experience of finding happiness in someone else's happiness because your love for them is so great. It has also been explained as the act of joyfully giving someone the chance of a positive experience, even if it results in you not having it.

Oodal (Tamil)
"Oodal" is the fake anger that couples tease each other with. Almost like a light form of banter, it's that exaggerated, often melodramatic anger

and sulking between lovers when they purposefully let themselves get offended (usually over something inconsequential) in an attempt to get the other to apologize first. It's done with affection and it's a way to playfully strengthen bonds.

Yugen (Japanese)
The Japanese have many important concepts of aesthetics as they relate to life and art, often one in the same. Yūgen is one of many worth exploring. Yūgen is an awareness of the universe that leaves you with emotions too deep and mysterious for words. Similar to the definition of the word "ineffable," "yūgen" refers to feelings and ideas too great or extreme to be expressed or described in words.

Using the idea of yūgen in writing:
"To contemplate the flight of wild geese seen and lost among the clouds."
-Zeami Motokiyo

Yūgen describes a depth of appreciation for this experience of life, one that sees and allows us to be one with all the ineffable and profound beauty of the universe as it presents itself, as well as the sad beauty of human suffering.

Dadirri (Australian aboriginal term)
"Dadirri" is a deep, spiritual act of quiet, reflective and respectful listening—a still awareness within. It's a tuning in, a reconnection experience with the specific aim to remember our deeper understanding of the beauty of nature. Dadirri recognizes the inner spirit that calls us to reflection and contemplation of the immense wonders of this creation.

Sukha (Sanskrit)

"Sukha" is genuine, lasting happiness, independent of circumstances. In Sanskrit and Pali, "suhka" means an authentic state of happiness, pleasure, ease, or bliss that has a lasting quality, compared to "preya" which is more of a transient pleasure. So "sukha" refers more to happiness with a comfort and a settled sense of ease to it. Regarding the function of our bodies, sukha means that everything is working together harmoniously. Here, comfort and ease may not always be appropriate descriptive words. Better definitions might be physical balance, homeostasis, and wellbeing. It's a kind of body equanimity.

Orenda (Iroquois)

"Orenda" is the Iroquois name for a spiritual energy inherent in people and their environment. Even storms are said to possess orenda—just stand outside and watch as a storm approaches. Feel its presence. It's a collective power of nature's energies through the living energy of all natural objects, animate and inanimate. It's an extraordinary invisible power believed to live in varying degrees in all animate and inanimate natural objects. It's a transmissible spiritual energy capable of being exerted according to the will of its possessor. A strong connection exists between prayers and songs and orenda: through song, a bird, shaman, all put forth orenda. Orenda describes the power of our volition as we relate to ourselves and our world—the ability of the human will to change the world in the face of the powerful forces surrounding them.

So that's my list. And make no mistake about it, there's a world of words, concepts, greetings, and forms of love to choose from on this planet! Make a list of your favorite words that you might like to have in

your life, or even try and work into your vocabulary. Try and own them, really explore their meanings so you resonate with their message.

> *Note:* To understand the essence of a word doesn't require you to memorize it or even use it. Simply having knowledge of it enables you to, in some way, embody it, to make it part of your life. Just be aware of its essence, its existence, and use that knowledge to support your life.

_____

_____

_____

_____

_____

_____

_____

POWER STATEMENT LOGBOOK

Jumping into the Game

Here's a little direction for finding your Power Statements. Try this thinking exercise to help you explore, build, and refine your list to draw from. As you ask yourself some of the simple questions below, open yourself up to all the possible directions you can go with them. Remember, it's an exercise of personal exploration. Give yourself permission to let anything and anyone be a potential catalyst to finding the triggers of inspiration hidden within you.

Do your best to answer some of these questions. It helps to have a pen and paper or note-taking device in hand. You can try and answer them all at once or just approach one a week. You can scan them all and just pick out the ones that strike your fancy, or hit the ones that make you nervous. It's your journey, do it how you want. But when an idea, word, or person pops in your head, it helps to write it down so you can explore when you want without having to memorize everything (which, in my mind, is just way too much work)!

- **What subjects do you love to talk about?**
  What feeds you? What can you not stop talking about once you get rolling? What do you fearlessly talk about with your most comfortable, trusted, and connected friend? Heart stuff? Body stuff? Intellectual concepts? A mixture of all of them? Do your best to make a list, write them down.
- **What and who inspires you?**
  Anything at all? Health concepts? Creativity, art, writing, invention? The motivation of others? Bravery? Courage? Children? The Olym-

pics? The Special Olympics? People stepping beyond adversity and making choices of strength in life? Those who have recognized their special gifts and embraced them? The story of an average Joe expanding past his/her social programing and finding their truth? People taking care of one another? Great feats of heroism? Little gifts of great love? Exploring any of these ideas or people can shed light on what it is to feed your own heart. Your time is well spent looking into all kinds of concepts, ideas, and people that reflect your own heart in some way.

- **What subjects are you hesitant to discuss with others and what do you just hate to talk about?**
Is there fear around it, and do you find yourself making yourself small because of it? Take a look at the things that scare or anger you—they're the subjects worth exploring, worth looking for the *why* behind them, and the wisdom hiding within the healing of our response to them.

- **What concepts tend to create judgment in your mind?**
Judgment. Pay attention here, peel your judgment apart, dissect it. Wherever our judgment pulls on us hardest reveals something of our greatest lessons. So don't avoid looking at the things that make you feel ugly. They are teachers for the eager student. There's always an opportunity for healing where judgment is addressed. We can always find wisdom and truth when we move beyond our judgment.

- **Who do you love? Who do you really really not love? And why?**
Just open up to the why, the reasons, the inspiration behind the good feeling as well as the repulsion, and write down the thinking that creates what you believe you feel.

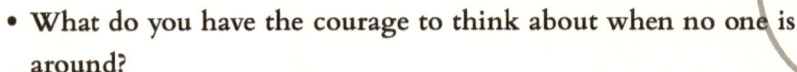

- **What do you have the courage to think about when no one is around?**
  What are the secrets of you, the freedom of the heart as it moves through you? What are the very personal messages here, or the healing being summoned through you?
- **What do you "wish" you could talk about freely?**
  Are there "taboo" subjects that we unnecessarily fear, or are there things that need to be explored and healed within?
- **Loved by society or not, which figures inspire you?**
  Look for the *why*. It's okay if it's Mother Theresa or Napoleon. But why? What is the strength or the truth these people inspire in your mind and heart?
- **Alive or dead, made-up or real, who are your greatest heroes?**
  Look for the *why*.
- **What feeds your heart, your mind, your most intense as well as your mildest interests in life?**
  Touch on what holds your attention—anything and everything if you want. This is your unique life, your *Power Statement Logbook*, put absolutely anything you want on your list of potentials for exploration and inspiration!

Take your time. Explore the words and concepts behind the questions that grab you. Give yourself the freedom to explore beyond what's easily seen, allow any boundaries to fade, and get into the grit of who you are.

All your answers, your words, or your phrases give you something to draw from. They're fuel for the journey, things to look at, po-

tentials for inspiration, reasons for change, and opportunities for growth. Without judgment or emotional attachment, explore your concepts, the people, or ideas that touch you. Open yourself to the good, the bad, and the ugly as you explore the nature of your relationship to the human condition. Even exploring your most negative concept is an exercise for potential healing when you do it with heart. When we're open, we can find ways that help us move away from our negativity or toxicity around it. Because if you know where the pain is, it's easier to treat the wound.

Make a list of things that really turn your gears in life—the people and concepts that really twists your piggies. You're looking for the ideas that spark your higher interest and touch your heart in some way. Refine the words that feed you and see what sticks, let them frame a picture in your mind you can draw from. Grab some paper, or your phone, and take a note. Create a list you can build on over time, you can get rid of it whenever you want, come back to it whenever the time is right, keep it in your desk, or just hold it in your pocket as your reminder. It's your personal freedom list—just do your best to make it work for you.

This is an example of how I explored silence and quiet—how I dug into a word and concept that's meaningful to me.

In my world, sitting quietly holds a lot of importance. It moves me, and I've always known that it helps me reset—to somehow freshen myself. Admittedly, I never really understood exactly what that need was about. I just knew that quiet and solitude was good for me, and it felt important to nurture.

It wasn't until I explored what others had to say about silence and quiet and what it meant to them that I was able to get a firmer grasp on it for myself. I explored quotes, read poems, listened to ideas, found and considered the antonyms and synonyms, read the book *Quiet* by Susan Cain, and simply took time to study and absorb the deeper words around this inner place of solitude I so loved. My research helped me uniquely define it for myself. Their words gave me permission to expand into my quiet, to appreciate my intuitive need for time spent in the presence and wisdom of silence.

Below are some quotes that I connected with. They showed me I was not alone, and, really, that I'm in pretty good company. These are a few examples of many that helped me cultivate a greater understanding and acceptance of my need for solitude and quiet. Quotes like these helped explain why I felt like I derive such strength and rejuvenation through silence and meditation. Not surprisingly, Albert Einstein and Rumi were favorites.

"The monotony and solitude of a quiet life stimulates the creative mind."
-Albert Einstein

"Silence is the sleep that nourishes wisdom."
-Francis Bacon

"Listen to silence. It has much to say."
-Rumi

"*Silence is a source of great strength.*"
-Lao Tzu

"*Silence, healing.*"
-Heraclitus

"*Solitude is a catalyst for innovation.*"
-Susan Cain

"*The quieter you become, the more you are able to hear.*"
-Rumi

"*Muddy water is best cleared by leaving it alone.*"
-Alan Watts

"*I never found the companion that was so companionable as solitude. We are for the most part more lonely when we go abroad among men than when we stay in our chambers.*"
-Henry David Thoreau

"*Everything has its wonders, even darkness and silence, and I learn whatever state I am in, therein to be content.*"
-Helen Keller

"*I think 99 times and find nothing. I stop thinking, swim in silence, and the truth comes to me.*"
-Albert Einstein

I also searched the antonyms and synonyms for silence and quiet. Here are some simple words that I felt a connection with.

Synonyms: calm, peaceful, soft, close, still
Antonyms: clamorous, noisy, agitation, unruly

Quiet: The Power of Introverts in a World That Can't Stop Talking
by Susan Cain

I found a friend in this book. It helped me to see and more deeply understand myself, to embrace why I walked through life in my unique way. Quiet helped me understand myself and be myself. The author had found greater understanding for her own world, and through a peak into her process, it helped me do the same for my own world.

I also saw Ms. Cain speak some years back at a venue in Grand Rapids. Being in the presence of someone who has done so much thinking on and research about the importance of following our need for quiet was validating in a way books could not impart. There was an energetic exchange that comes from being in the same room with someone who connects with your heart. This was another link in the chain of accepting myself and finding my greater balance.

ROSCOE

Note: You don't always have to go to such extremes with the concepts you want to explore. Sometimes a simple quote might suffice, or finding an idea that the mind can gain a little understanding through. With quiet and silence, I simply found myself drawn to and immersed in the subject and its power, so I went with it. And I'm still drawn in. I still find myself exploring it often. It seems like there's always a new bit of gold to be found—a little more truth to be had for the journey.

Simple Power Statements

Simple Power Statements are just that. They're the easy to understand words, phrases, and ideas that present a truth that extends beyond their simplicity. They help us build a framework within that creates a structure of strength, one that only requests and requires the attention of the heart.

Create a list of your simplest Power Statements.
Example:
    "I am..."
    "I am love."
    "Allow"
    "Listen"
    "Listen to the whisper."

-
-
-
-
-
-

Part Two
Ideas of Power

Power Statement
ANTIDOTES
for feeling emotionally stuck

You're human, and you're likely to experience all kinds of emotions throughout your day. It's estimated that we have somewhere between 50,000 and 100,000 thoughts a day. There's got to be a bunch of everything in there—all kinds of thinking that reflects your broad life experience, and a lot of it is brightened or shadowed with emotion. It might pop out as a strong, overwhelming emotion, or as just a whisper, but it's definitely there, influencing the quality of those 50,000+ thoughts.

Potentially, your thinking colors your world in good ways and bad. The bad or negative and pain-inducing thinking can disrupt you to the core, it can rock you to a point where living from your heart becomes impossible. When you come across these moments, try and clarify them, identify the emotions that have shaken you, try to put words to the feelings that influence your thinking.

Working an emotion like this helps in the process of finding and healing the quality of our thinking and the emotions that hold us. When you can define the emotion(s) that caused the break in your healthy flow of thought—recognize what created the disruption and its influence on how you're experiencing life—it sets you up for a healing process that allows you to shift into new, fresher thought if you choose. Identification and release can set you up to briefly pause, to give yourself a moment to explore without attachment to the emotion presenting itself, where it's coming from, and perhaps even look at its origination, or explore beyond it.

To examine the full energy of an emotionally charged moment is important if you want to explore yourself for the antidote to that emotion. It helps to find the word, phrase, or feeling that helps you participate in your own healing process and helps shifts you back toward the powerful strength of your heart.

At my clinic, we do a lot body-mind or mind-body work, releasing the aberrant emotional charges held in the physical body. And as I'm working with people, we're trying to define the emotions that might be causing any disruption to the body-mind balance. In the technique, we're able to identify negative emotions, like frustration, resentment, or low self-worth, to name a few, and once we've found an active disruptive emotional complex, I'll often ask patients to sit with it for a minute. I ask them to quietly explore within themselves the emotion they're stuck in and open to the antidote to that emotion. I ask them to look for the word or phrase that counteracts the troubled emotion so that it might have an avenue to heal.

As they explore for the antidote, I might lead them a bit, asking them, for example, "What is the emotion that frees you of that frustration, or what opens your heart to self-love, and how can you step past it? What quality of thinking do you need to hold in order to release your resentment?" Then I leave them to their process as I go to another patient. When I come back, they've almost always found their antidote in a word, phrase, or idea—a unique way to see and think differently about their issue. It's usually quite a surprise to me because it's so uniquely theirs, not what I might have expected, but it's always eye-opening for them as well as myself.

This is what I want you to do. I want you to explore for the antidotes to your glitchy emotional blocks in life; to find ways of healing that can flow through you.

Emotions We Hold,
and the Antidotes That Can Help to Release Them

In the "Emotional Overlay Technique," a technique we use in my clinic to determine what emotion is interfering with our healthy thought, or what concepts are negatively impacting our overall wellbeing, we understand that the body is made to follow the mind, so it's reasonable that the body will hold the charge of a negative, harmful, or disruptive emotion. It's equally reasonable to expect that the body wants to find health and balance, and therefore is "willing" to help identify where the aberrant charges might be held so that they can be approached, identified, and neutralized. We all really want to be healthy. As a practitioner of natural healing techniques, it's a matter of learning how to accurately read the body and listen to what it's saying so that we can find and use the information that we need to help it find its balance.

Emotions are complex, and sometimes having a simple, even small explanation helps us integrate with them better, it helps us understand them on a different and more life-real level. And with greater understanding, it helps us see why we get stuck in their grasp so completely. It's all part of this human journey—dealing with our emotions and understanding them. The definitions that follow are meant to help us integrate with our emotions better and incorporate them into our human condition. Because that condition really can be difficult to navigate. A little explanation goes a long way for us, giving us permission to feel and move through our emotions as an essential part of our healing.

Next is a list of potential emotions that we tend to get caught up in. They're examples of different emotions I commonly explore with patients while doing Emotional Overlay Technique. Take a minute and read through some of them. You're bound to find areas where you get stuck. Take advantage of the feelings that come up and explore what it is to find a Power Statement that effectively takes any destructive charge down a notch or two.

Each emotion comes with simple descriptions that can be expanded to suit your personal needs if necessary. These are the emotions that are commonly activated within us and can overwhelm our lives. Underneath each emotion is an antidote to that emotion: a word or concept that helps us release the charge of the difficult emotion. Antidotes can be Power Statements, words, actions, concepts, or ideas. I use words that help reclaim my wellbeing, words and phrases that help reestablish my belonging and my natural state of presence in life. This list is very similar to the words and concepts I might use when I work with patients.

Note: As we explore these emotions and antidotes, our attention is on how these words and concepts are held within our hearts and bodies. Though their descriptions might not be dictionary perfect, we're trying to create a picture in the mind around how they might be impacting the disruption of healing in our body and our mind in our human experience.

Additionally: Whereas a recognized painful emotion might tend to be very specific, antidotes are more broad in their application. A single antidote can apply to many different emotions. For example, gratitude is a universal healer. It has the capacity to act as an antidote for anything, from anger to worry. It can touch everything in a healing way. The same can be said for the healing of antidotes like love, forgiveness, compassion, kindness, as well as phrases like, "There are no human enemies, there are just people in pain asking for help." All of these can be used as antidotes for our attachment to multiple difficult emotions.

The Emotional Short List

Overly Sympathetic *(sympathy to a fault, a depleting sympathy)*
Feeling overly sympathetic is similar to feeling sorry for yourself, your situation, or feeling sorry for others and their situations. It's simply going overboard on the sympathy boat (losing yourself in your reaction through pity, commiseration, and sorrow while absorbing the difficulty), rather than approaching yourself or others with strong and healthy empathy (being understanding, compassionate, and appreciating the difficulty of a situation without having to take it on emotionally). In overly sympathetic mode, we relate from a point of weakness, a kind of pouting approach, rather than relating form a healthy internal stance. With empathy, we approach situations and leave them in a stance of strength, we cultivate systems of self-respect and self-belief. An overly sympathetic approach tends to create an environment of low self-worth and lack of belief in oneself or others—an approach that's pleading for an antidote.

Antidotes: Understanding and using healthy empathy. Believing in ourselves or one another as strong and capable. Embracing a healthy self-love, the belief in yourself and others, and standing with a self-worth that doing your best is enough. Knowing everything has a deep purpose we may or may not understand, and our job is to be alive to it.

I can also choose antonyms like: Healthy empathy, understanding, believing in the strength of another, blessings…

Explore the meaning behind quotes like:
*"If we take man as he is, we make him worse.
If we take man as he should be, we make him capable of what he can be."*
-Viktor Frankl

*"I think if you allow yourself to mope and feel sorry for yourself,
it can take years off your life."*
-Norman Lloyd

*"Our human compassion binds us to one another - not in pity
or patronizingly, but as human beings who have learned how
to turn our common suffering into hope for the future."*
-Nelson Mandela

*"Compassion does not just happen. Pity does, but compassion is not pity.
It's not a feeling. Compassion is a viewpoint, a way of life, a perspective, a
habit that becomes a discipline - and more than anything else, compassion is
a choice we make that love is more important than comfort or convenience."*
-Glennon Doyle Melton

*"Many of life's problems and sorrows are inevitable,
but feeling sorry for yourself is a choice."*
-Amy Morin

Expanded Self-Importance

When we're stuck in a state of expanded self-importance, it's expressed as overt over-concern with ourselves, stuck in the me-me-me-what-about-me-hands-on-hips-how-about-my-needs syndrome. It's the "embiggening" of ourselves (as Homer Simpson liked to put it). It's an inner stance that's quite reminiscent of being stuck in the I, ME, and MINE, represented in Buddhism. When you're stuck in an expanded importance of self, you've copped an attitude of needing to prove your case in things, not be wrong, even before you fully listen to what others are trying to say.

Before going into a sweat lodge that I attended years back, the leader gave a whole talk about how we tend to walk around in "self-importance," disrupting our own journey, and creating a toxic environment for ourselves. Expanded importance of self and the self-importance he was talking about are mirrors to each other. Both require that you put yourself above or below others, and both require you to get stuck in your personal concerns while expecting others to go down that road with you. It's an interaction quagmire when it comes to connecting with others with strength and grace. You can't see past yourself and, therefore, you can't see clearly. Synonyms might be: arrogant, cocky, pompous, presumptuous, conceited, or vain.

Antidotes: Understand the concept: no one above and no one below (you're not better or more important than anybody, and no one is better or more important than you). When you understand this, you understand that we are all equal, all doing our best, and that, for the most part, there are simply people like ourselves, in struggle, trying to find their heart.

POWER STATEMENT LOGBOOK

I can also choose antonyms like: Humility, reverential, unassuming, unpretentious, without airs, natural, straightforward, open, honest, sincere...

Explore the meaning behind quotes like:
"There are times when wisdom cannot be found in the chambers of parliament or the halls of academia but at the unpretentious setting of the kitchen table."
-E.A. Bucchianeri

"Don't be arrogant, because arrogance kills curiosity and passion."
-Mina Bissell

"When people unfortunately use religion to facilitate their envy, arrogance and hate, communalism surfaces."
-Radhanath Swami

Living Your Life Through Others *(Experiencing what you believe to be your own life by vicariously over participating in someone else's.)*

"You care so much you feel as though you will bleed to death with the pain of it."
-J.K. Rowling

This is living the life that was meant for you, not for yourself, but through what another does or needs. We do this in normal parenting to an extent, but it's unhealthy when taken to extremes, pretty much with anyone else. Here, the concern for another takes us over and our life

gets directed by their success or failure, we end up living through others' needs and relationships, giving up living our lives through our own center—our life is designated to another. These days, it can even be the result of an addiction to social media, living life through watching someone else's life experiences, as though it somehow completes our life. Overall, it's a giving up of our sense of self to outside relationships.

Antidotes: Living from your center, reclaiming your inner stance, connecting with your presence, reclaiming your life, exploring self-love, stepping back and redefining healthy relationships, believing in others to succeed, knowing that others are capable and meant to take care of themselves, knowing that you can be next to someone without sacrificing your sense of self.

I can also choose antonyms like: Reclaiming your own power, reclaiming your inner stance, living authenticly, living first-hand, being in your life...

Explore the meaning behind quotes like:
"Don't ever live vicariously. This is your life. Live."
-Lavinia Spalding

"It is easier to live through someone else than to complete yourself. The freedom to lead and plan your own life is frightening if you have never faced it before. It is frightening when a woman (a person) finally realizes that there is no answer to the question 'who am I' except the voice inside herself (themself)."
-Betty Friedan

POWER STATEMENT LOGBOOK

Grief

"No one ever told me that grief felt so like fear."
-C.S. Lewis

Grief is intense mental suffering or distress over affliction or loss, sharp sorrow, or painful regret. Grief is a powerful emotion for many people—sometimes their biggest. It's common to the human condition and can be overwhelming to our state of wellbeing. Grief leaves us in a cavern of deep agony and anguish, impacting the hearts of those experiencing it. Grief comes to us for various reasons: when life just isn't turning out the way you thought it would, you can feel grief around it, with any type of loss, whether it be a marriage, a loved one, a pet or companion, not to mention the loss of a dream, as well as material loss, there comes different qualities of grief. The loss of a job or position in life can activate feelings of being less than, there's huge grief felt over the loss of our sense of self. Grief is quite naturally felt with any loss, and it can take us over. Our job is to handle it with compassion and understanding and not get stuck in its layers of toxicity.

I've watched as people experienced heartbreak because they were told they should avoid eating bread, sweets, or milk products due to a dietary sensitivity, in despair, exclaiming, "I could never give up my ice cream at night," or, "I could never live like that!" They say it even though they know their food choices are literally killing them. But it causes grief, because it's about the loss, not the logic, and it can feel too painful to bear. In that, we become rigid in our thinking and sometimes refuse to lovingly take care of ourselves and see the abundance in our lives.

Antidotes: So, of course, a clear antidote is to bring feelings of gratitude into the mix; to allow ourselves to acknowledge all the blessings we have besides the pain—cultivating an appreciation for all that we've been given, and understanding that everything in life is purposefully made to be temporary.

Understand that there's a gift beyond the wound, and whatever the losses may be, whatever you've had to endure, it's an example of life unfolding. Know that the huge potential and abundance, peace, and a joy in life always surrounds you—that you only need to open your eyes and your heart to it.

I can also choose antonyms like: Blessing, contentedness, joy, peace, calm and hopeful...

Explore the meaning behind quotes like:
"Grief can be the garden of compassion. If you keep your heart open through everything, your pain can become your greatest ally in your life's search for love and wisdom."
-Rumi

"Don't grieve. Anything you lose comes round in another form."
-Rumi

"Grief does not change you, Hazel. It reveals you."
-John Green

Compelled to Neatness *(The compulsive need to control something in one's environment.)*

We want to define "compelled to neatness" beyond the obvious compulsion to straighten pictures, vacuum, and tidy up books. Being stuck in the phrase "compelled to neatness" also denotes getting caught up in a frantic or compulsive need to organize many other aspects of our life; the need to micromanage our world, people and their behavior, and it can come across as an intolerance to the lifestyle of others because they don't think or act as we think they should. Being compelled to neatness can be observed as rigidly organizing our time or the events in our life to fit into a particular box. It's seen in our compulsive need for more money, as well as our need to accommodate everybody's needs and demands, regardless of the effect it has on us. We find ourselves saying what's deemed appropriate rather than what's true, strong, and honest.

People usually have several responses when the emotional component of "compelled to neatness" comes up. They'll say, "Yeah, I'm pretty persnickety about things!" or, "Yup, I need everything in place, especially the people around me! I don't keep things neat and tidy, but I sure need people to do things and act in certain ways." We can get very nit-picky about how we do things, or how others act. So, we function in life, compelled to make sure that everything is done externally and internally exactly the way we demand. Being compelled to neatness, we just can't let things be, and we've got to control it! And yes, it's exhausting to the heart of us!

Antidotes: Our first step is recognizing when we're stuck in "compelled to neatness." After that, it's a matter of finding our new stance and creat-

ROSCOE

ing some words around it. We need to consciously let go of the need to control, and find greater understanding around phrases like, "Everything is just as it needs to be," or, "It is what it is," or, "This is not ours," and, "There's no need to fret over this." I like to use phrases like, "It's just a thought," and, "I can let this settle," or, "I probably don't need to chew on this anymore, I can set this aside." And when I feel like I need to do everything I'm asked or even not asked, it's, "Be free of the good opinions of others," or, "I just need to mind my own business." Find what works best for you.

I can also choose antonyms like: Liberation from the habits of a controlling mind, understanding it's just thought (when you feel the compulsion to control something), and I can let this settle (rather than micromanaging). I probably don't need to chew on this anymore. I can set this aside…

Explore the meaning behind quotes like:
Personally, I like to say to myself when I'm nitpicky about life: "*You've already won the race, stop fussing over the details!*"

"I don't let myself get upset about the little nitpicky things anymore."
-Eric Shanteau

"Having no need to judge, control, react, so forgiveness does not even arise."
-Jay Woodman

"You like to claim that you're in charge of the world, but it's as if the world hasn't noticed and it does whatever it pleases in spite of you. You claim the sky is blue, but almost on a daily basis it betrays you."
-Trish Mercer

The Sense of Dread

Before an adjustment, a patient was looking at one of my wall charts on emotion. He was very curious about the concept of an emotional overlay and its impact on the body. I explained that an overlay happens when we hold an unresolved and difficult emotion within the body and it creates dysfunction and disruption to our state of wellbeing. I explained that it can potentially impact our health on all levels: body, mind, as well as spirit. He wanted to experiment, to see if he had any of these "emotional overlays." So I tested him on a coworker he said he was struggling with, and we found the emotion of dread. No sooner did we find it that he chimed in with an enthusiastic, "Yes! That's exactly what I feel every time I walk into the room with this guy. It's been exhausting!" We all know what it is to have a sense of dread about something or someone. Dreading seeing our ex-spouse, dreading the IRS audit, dreading going to the dentist. We all have something that we dread in an almost terrifying way, and we often turn it into something bigger than it is, we give it too much of our life, leaving us feeling horrible. It's never worth it.

Antidotes: The antidote for a sense of dread depends on the quality of that dread. It helps to understand that most everything in life is temporary and believing in yourself to get through them. Understanding that you're safe and that external experiences should never be given the power over your internal state of wellbeing. In this world, you are a welcome traveler, accepted and strong, and you can always choose greater ease, even in the difficult situations you are, indeed, dreading. Trust in your strength and character, and refuse to allow situations to dictate your life. Since dread is a quality of fear that paralyzes our very movement, freeing yourself from it is the act of giving yourself permission to be alive to your life. It's the

ROSCOE

gift of being present to the aliveness of your new-now rather than caught up in the stale drama of your old fears.

I can also choose antonyms like: Contentedness, happiness, pleasant, pleasing, peace, welcomed, wonderful, accepted, ease, calm...

Explore the meaning behind quotes like:

"It's funny, the moment you dread the most, seeing yourself bald, is actually not such a bad moment at all."
-Sylvie Meis

"It isn't what you have or who you are or where you are or what you are doing that makes you happy or unhappy. It is what you think about it."
-Dale Carnegie

"Because one believes in oneself, one doesn't try to convince others. Because one is content with oneself, one doesn't need others' approval. Because one accepts oneself, the whole world accepts him or her."
-Lao Tzu

"For after all, the best thing one can do when it is raining is let it rain."
-Henry Wadsworth Longfellow

"Be content with what you have; rejoice in the way things are. When you realize there is nothing lacking, the whole world belongs to you."
-Lao Tzu

POWER STATEMENT LOGBOOK

Contemplative Consumption

This is when we're obsessively reflective, ruminating in our minds, even to the point of being pensive or consumed in our thought. Simply put, being stuck in contemplative consumption is being stuck in your head about activities, problems (real or imagined), and caught up the emotional and social challenges of life. It's when we're stuck strongly in our head about almost any aspect of life—feeling like your noggin is trapped in continuous contemplative thought, rather than being alive to the moment, and connected to your heart. In contemplative consumption, you're chewing, chewing, chewing on your thinking, whatever it might be. Your brain never seems to take a break, and you are certainly deaf to your hearts whisper. It can be a specific issue, or can feel like everything! People really know when they're stuck here, and when it comes up, they almost always say something like, "Yeah, it's horrible. I feel like I can't turn my brain off. I'm constantly thinking about things that either have no importance or things I wish I could let go of." It's nervous contemplative thought with no productive outcome.

Antidotes: The use of heart-centered breathing helps calm the frantic, overly contemplative mind. Be present to your breath while placing attention on the heart. Allow the mind to hold thoughts of appreciation and gratitude while releasing from its attachments. There's a learned art to letting go of things that we have no control over. It plays an essential roll in freeing ourselves from compulsive overthinking. Additionally, understanding that all things in life are very simply temporary gives us permission to let them settle away.

Know that many of the worries we get stuck in are actually

products of the past and they don't really exist anymore, or they're part of our future fear, which doesn't exist either. Understanding this allows us to release ourselves from these prisons we make in our mind. Allowing the past to be past, and not living in an irrational fear over a future that hasn't and may never happen helps us question the sanity of giving fear so much power over our precious now, our presence, our life. It allows us the freedom to be truly alive to our lives.

Living the "Don't worry about it" life.
If there's a difficulty and no solution, let it go.
If there's a solution, awesome. Work it, and chill out.
If there's no problem, well then, why worry?

I can also choose antonyms like: Peace, your relaxed mind, being at ease, allowing life to simply be and to be simpler, mindful, awake, presence...

Explore the meaning behind quotes like:

"Writer: It's not an occupation; it's a compulsion."
-Teresa Nielsen Hayden

"Compulsion is the death of friendship, joy."
-Patrick O'Brian,

"For every minute you are angry you lose sixty seconds of happiness."
-Ralph Waldo Emerson

"Count your age by friends, not years. Count your life by smiles, not tears."
-John Lennon

Impending Doom

Do you ever find yourself walking through life waiting for the bottom to drop out? It could be about a particular topic, it might be everything, or just your wiring in this moment. Regardless, you're just marking time until things fall apart. The kids, work, the economy, relationships, the house, plumbing, cars, finance, the weather, or simply all of the above. Well, that's living life in impending doom. We can find ourselves walking through our lives knowing that something's going to go wrong—you're like Chicken Little just waiting for the sky to fall and the poop to hit the fan. Impending doom.

We can get caught up in the habit of being in constant worry about life not working out, and usually it's about things we have absolutely no real control over. It might be about everything, which is a huge burden to carry, or you might have your favorites, your "specialized burdens." But nonetheless, you're stuck in your head, obsessively waiting for disaster and failure, with no productive end whatsoever. It's a waste of you.

Antidotes: Explore antidotes that create a release into an internal freedom, an appreciation of being present to your life now. Concepts like: finding your sense of calm, trusting in the unfolding/the process of life, and learning to live through a sense of collectedness, balance, or equanimity (a full life journey within itself). It's understanding that everything is as it should be, and it's about being patient with yourself, knowing that given your life experience so far, you're doing your best. Grasping that there's no need to worry about the future, the past, or any of the things we have no control over (and we don't have control over much). So quit

ROSCOE

making yourself miserable over impending doom. Take a breath, find the precious moment, and stop putting your life on hold. Just be here now!

Note: Equanimity is a state of wellbeing which is undisturbed by our outer experience. In a state of equanimity, we remain largely unaffected by our exposure to emotions, pain, distractions, or difficulties that can typically disrupt the harmony of the mind. In equanimity, we maintain a resiliency to our environment, retaining a balanced state of wellbeing, even in disruptive situations. It's here where our circumstances no longer define the quality of our experience.

I can also choose antonyms like: Calm, trust, hope, courage, collected, collectedness, rational, logical…

Explore the meaning behind quotes like:
"Have enough courage to trust love one more time and always one more time."
-Maya Angelou

"None of us knows what might happen even the next minute, yet still we go forward. Because we trust. Because we have Faith."
-Paulo Coelho

"I'm not saying that putting on makeup will change the world or even your life, but it can be a first step in learning things about yourself you may never have discovered otherwise. At worst, you could make a big mess and have a good laugh."
-Kevyn Aucoin

POWER STATEMENT LOGBOOK

*"Just try new things. Don't be afraid.
Step out of your comfort zones and soar, all right?"*
-Michelle Obama

*"The first step toward success is taken when you refuse to be
a captive of the environment in which you first find yourself."*
-Mark Caine

Emotionally Repressed

When we're feeling emotionally repressed, we're actually stuck in our head and away from our heart. We can't seem to let ourselves feel the emotions flowing through us, and we certainly don't want anyone else to see them either. We're just not willing to wake up to being fully alive. It's a denial of our emotional body and, really, it's a denial of our truth. Our emotions are there, but we push them back, they feel too vulnerable, difficult, confusing, or painful, and we psychologically can't allow ourselves to take the risk of expressing them. We're unable to see why it would serve us to explore them, much less feel them.

Repressing ourselves emotionally happens when we feel overwhelmed with the dynamics of being human. And we end up stuck in anger, depression, aggression, and grief, to name a few, where overwhelm with that emotion leaves us in shut down mode. Emotionally, we become fearful of feeling the intensity of being vulnerable and being human. It's a place where we never learn from our experiences because the emotions are never allowed to teach us their lessons. When we're stuck feeling emotionally repressed, we might feel dulled to life, detached from our-

selves. Feeling when we've resisted it is a tough place to begin a journey, but we need to give ourselves permission to feel, and to be more fully human. It's that journey out of the head and into the heart. It reflects our very being.

Antidote: Give yourself permission to feel, to open to life. Know that moving through something is far more productive to you than denying yourself. Trust yourself to process your life in a healthy way. Free your human identity to come forward. And like Terence in *Heauton Timorumenos* says, "I am human, and I think nothing human is alien to me."

I can also choose antonyms like: Allow yourself to feel, opening to life, opening to the truth of things...

Explore the meaning behind quotes like:
"The tragedy of life is in what dies inside a man while he lives - the death of genuine feeling, the death of inspired response, the awareness that makes it possible to feel the pain or the glory of other men in yourself."
–Norman Cousins

"Get outside. Watch the sunrise. Watch the sunset. How does that make you feel? Does it make you feel big or tiny? Because there's something good about feeling both."
–Amy Grant

Irrational Feelings and Thoughts

These are the feelings and thoughts that seem to come out of nowhere and are void of rational reasoning. We've all had them in times of stress, when we have no idea how to handle a situation, and we've come up with thoughts that just don't always make sense. They might be based in magical thinking, worst case scenario and catastrophic thought, paranoia, and leaps of logic that just don't seem rational. Irrationality can cover a broad range of dysfunctional thinking, but once you can label and dissect an irrational thought, you take away some of its power. You can bring a little sanity to a troubled way of thinking.

There can be group irrationality, where everyone agrees to believe in a similar idea or even delusion. We may not see it because we're too invested, but the people around us that aren't involved would. Irrational thinking is a quality of thinking that begins in our head and should stop there. We should head it off and put it to rest, but we don't. For some reason, we feel the need to believe in it. It's thinking deprived of reason. The thinking that, deep down, if we pay attention, we usually know is somehow off center—ideas that seem good and right in the moment, but with time and reflection it becomes obvious they're not based in clear thought.

Antidote: Avoid making assumptions. And fully explore any belief system you chose to follow. Question yourself about the truth of any issue before you fire up the engines of assumption, judgment, or negative thought. Ask yourself if you're in a right state of mind to even be considering a particular topic of interest. Make sure you're completely clear about things before you move forward, giving yourself to an idea.

Assumptions cultivate irrational thinking, but cultivating the questions that lead to clear thought breaks their power. So, always look for and wait on clarity.

When asking yourself questions, try to put a new and different perspective on it, give new thought permission to evolve. Ask yourself questions like, "If a friend explained this same issue to me, how would I handle it/respond? What might I think? What would I tell them?" Courageously question yourself, "If I stand back from this idea or comment, am I really making sense?" or, "What is the truth of this?" Try to stay open, looking for the higher truth of any topic. Is it kind, is it loving, is it helpful?

I can also choose antonyms like: Realistic, question the quality of your thinking, rational approaches, is this a loving thought, reflective wisdom, and opening to a sense of safe secure wellbeing...

Explore the meaning behind quotes like:

"Beware the irrational, however seductive."
-Christopher Hitchens

"To irrational principles, one cannot be loyal. Ideas that are not derived from reality cannot be consistently practiced in reality."
-Ayn Rand

"We believe certain things because they ought to be true."
-Thomas Gilovich, *How We Know What Isn't So: The Fallibility of Human Reason in Everyday Life*

Frustration, Annoyance, Irritation

The mother of all other emotions! It's a feeling of dissatisfaction, one that can incorporate other emotions like anxiety, anger, or depression, to name a few. Frustration usually results from our unfulfilled needs or unresolved problems. And who in this world has never felt frustration at some level, whether it's from something lame like not being able to open a bag of chips, or a loved one making really bad choices? I've gotten frustrated just trying to write about frustration! It's an easily accessible emotion for people. Frustration has the ability to infiltrate the breadth of our human experience. We're vulnerable to it, and we can tap into frustration just through thinking that something might not work out, contemplating something of the past, future, or simply through making up challenging scenarios in our mind. Before we know it, we're stuck in the emotion of our thinking, we're dancing with frustration.

As we said, we can slide into any unresolved emotion we have when the intensity of frustration takes over: anger, depression, sadness, grief, low self-worth, disgust, or fear, just to name a few, are all given their opportunity to move through us when we're stuck in frustration. Being overwhelmed with frustration opens us up to all our other potentials of emotion. It kind of explains why there's so much stress in the world! Life comes with its frustrations and if we let them get out of hand, our world follows suit in a multitude of ways. Sometimes I wonder if it would be more appropriate to call us "human frustrations" rather than "human beings!"

Overwhelming frustration can open all other doors of any kind of emotional attachment, but knowing that our primary emotion is that

"we're just feeling frustrated" gives us a tool, it allows us to put some of our struggle into context, to see through the eyes of being frustrated first, understanding that, even though we're scathing in anger or completely depressed, frustration may have been the primary trigger. It can take the charge of the associated emotion down a peg or two by simply saying to yourself, "I'm just feeling frustrated right now." Something inside of us allows us to accept that as a rather temporary emotion that we can let settle rather than allow ourselves to be defined by.

Antidote: When intense frustration comes up for us, it's helpful when we can sit back from our overwhelm and say to ourselves something like, "Oh, I'm just frustrated. I can let go of this," or, "It's the nature of this to settle." We simply need to find a way to give frustration permission to ease up, and it's all in the quality of our thinking around it. Acknowledging what it is creates a release, because, suddenly, the emotion doesn't look so big, uncontrollable, and overpowering. Knowing we're just frustrated helps us put our feelings in a place where we can choose to let go. Suddenly, we have something we can do with it. Suddenly, we can step back and say, "This could simply be me frustrated with life right now, I can work through that."

I can also choose antonyms like: Being open to trusting life, it is what it is, acceptance, releasing from anxious attachments, understanding, open-mindedness, smooth-headed, calm-minded...

Explore the meaning behind quotes like:
"A sense of humor is God's antidote for anger and frustration."
-Rick Warren

"Did you ever notice how difficult it is to argue with someone who is not obsessed with being right?"
–Wayne Dyer

"Never fret at any imperfections that you fear may impede your progress."
–Og Mandino

"The more positive emotions you feel, the happier you are. On the other hand, the more you indulge in negative emotions like anger and frustration, the unhappier you are."
–Maximilian Weigand

"How we decide to react to what is thrown at us is what determines our level or happiness or frustration."
–Folorunsho Mejabi

Lost and Vulnerable

Feeling lost and vulnerable might be described as feeling unprotected, disoriented, adrift, feeling bewildered or unsafe in every day life and open to moral attack, criticism, physical harm, undue anger and emotions from others, insecurity about environmental sensitivity, such as pollutants, even personal temptation. We walk through the world feeling weakened and easily taken advantage of, susceptible to being wounded or hurt. When this overwhelm, anguish, loss, or pain touches us, and we feel lost and unsure in our world, the result is that we move through our lives not knowing exactly what to do or how to feel safe and comfortable again. And in our vulnerable state (which we all feel at different times), we easily

feel the burn of the past and fear the potential pain of life in the future. We feel lost in our own skin, and we all too easily forget how strong we actually are. It's as though we've given something of ourselves away…

Antidote: Stand up and reclaim your personal power. Consistently claim your life, as many times and for as long as you need. Understand that your strength and resiliency is more than you're aware and it already resides within you. Stop justifying your worry, pull yourself back to the present. Vulnerability usually exists in the past or in future fears. Remember to be here now, and no matter what happens, there's always a deeper purpose behind it—lessons to be learned. So embrace your now, and be mindful of what life's offering you. Choose to live in what supports your life: happiness, truth, compassion, love, courage, reverence for life, appreciation and gratitude, non-violence, understanding, and self-love. Notice the hidden gift of yourself, and shed light on it. Remember that you're not a mistake and this life was meant for you. We all feel vulnerable in moments, however, we are also powerful beyond measure, and to find our truth in that is simply part of our journey of life. So again, reclaim your power. It's your right.

I can also choose antonyms like: An internal sense of security, strength, courage, and confidence, feeling safe…

Explore the meaning behind quotes like:
"I spent a lot of years trying to outrun or outsmart vulnerability by making things certain and definite, black and white, good and bad. My inability to lean into the discomfort of vulnerability limited the

fullness of those important experiences that are wrought with uncertainty: Love, belonging, trust, joy, and creativity to name a few."
–Brene Brown

"PTSD occurs following a trauma that was so awful that in retrospect you don't understand how you survived. What that causes is an extreme feeling of vulnerability that you get past but that doesn't go away."
–Mark Goulston

"We can appear to be tough as nails, but guys have a level of insecurity and vulnerability that's exponentially bigger than you think. With the primal urge to be alpha comes extreme heartbreak. The harder we fight, the harder we fall."
–John Krasinski

"I think one of the reasons I've had success in hip-hop is that I can bring out vulnerability in people who are generally seen as tough guys. To me, when a hip-hop musician always plays tough, I find it annoying because I know they're not really like that - there's something deeper and vulnerable. There has to be, because they're human beings."
–Skylar Grey

Needless to say, there are many, many more emotions to explore. Shame, despair, worry, hopelessness, paranoia, insecurity, resentment and anger, arrogance, and embarrassment are just a few to consider. We can potentially attach to all of these, and they will, indeed, end up depleting us. So find what sparks you and go explore their definitions and their impacts on our lives. Make notes of the antidotes that can help make these emotions less of a drama and trauma for us, and more just a thought that asks for our understanding.

Antidotes Made Simple

1. Do your best to identify the emotion of interest, meaning whatever best describes what you feel stuck in—the feeling, concept, or question with a negative charge—and do your best to put a name to what you're experiencing.

2. Named or not, pay attention to how it's attaching. Where do you feel it in your body? What kind of an energy does it generate within you? What or who does it make you think about?

3. Find your about-face, your release words, phrases or ideas for a particularly bad habit of the mind or struggle of the heart. Seek out the emotional antidote that helps recalibrate you and bring you back to a healthier sense of yourself and a deeper sense of your inner balance. This can be any healing word, phrase, or concept that effectively gets you unstuck and moving—one that releases you on some level from the original emotion—whether you can specifically name it or you just recognize the feeling it leaves you with.

4. Now connect with your antidote as many times as you need to in order to recreate a release of the mind and heart. Set up your mind and heart as though what you desire has already happened. This guides you into effectively discharging the power of whatever original difficult emotion has hold over your experience of being alive. It helps you heal your thinking, helps you remember your beauty.

Listening for Power STATEMENTS
hearing with your heart

A patient of mine, Bob, mentioned that his wife said to him, out of pure frustration for the tension they always seemed to be feeling in their lives, "And this! This is supposed to be the best time of our lives?"

It was a profound statement for him to hear, and he held on to the intention behind the question. As soon as he heard it, he knew it was meant to direct him. It turned into his Power Statement at that moment. Just the question of how to spend the best-time-of-life money (the retirement fund) caused him into re-evaluate the way he was living, where he was putting his importance. It was a hint received from his wife through a frustrated off-hand comment. But it meant more to Bob. He heard the message loud and clear. It was at that point Bob decided he was going to make whatever time they had left in this world worth it; that the rest of their lives would be "the best time of their lives," and he commented that it always should've been.

They didn't have much money, but they both more than made up for their lack of finances with their attitudes. They set their minds and hearts up to see the abundance of life surrounding them every day. They knew they had everything they needed to be happy, and when they did feel stressed, they chose to reevaluate their thinking, they looked for the solutions, antidotes, and qualities of thinking that helped move them into a state of wellbeing that reflected "the best time of their lives."

Bob was listening. And both he and Jackie caught wind of that little epiphany flying by, and they used it. They grabbed on to some inspired truth, found through playfully whining with each other about life, and they made it work for them—they made their lesson work for them. Life is a temporary thing, and we all have just one shot to run around the track. They found themselves asking: *Why not make this the best time of our lives? What are we waiting for? Why not embrace each of life's moments as new, fresh, and wonderful whenever we get the opportunity? Why not live in the abundance life is offering us right now?* And they lived a little more happily ever after, with plenty more lessons to come… because life is how it is.

We Hear First with Our Heart, it Helps Us Feed Our Mind.

Your heart is always paying attention to what's happening. Around and within you, your heart is listening. It hears all the rumbles of life as it flows through you, it brings a spark of attention to what moves you, and it communicates with its unmistakable whisper what's most important for you to know in life. Your heart's always listening, and it only asks you to listen back for its quiet wisdom.

Power Statements Help Us Remember Our Strength

I think the best Power Statement I've ever heard was from a twenty-one-year-old mother coming into my clinic for that dreaded baby-car-seat-low-back syndrome.

"I just decided to change the way I thought about my life."

I try to work closely with all my patients, putting effort into knowing them on a deeper, personal level. It helps me understand them as well as their health issues better and gives me some pretty good indicators as to where they might be physically as well as emotionally stuck. Either way, it relates to the overall wellbeing of the individual, so I ask a lot of questions about what brought them into the office as well as who they are and what their life has been like.

One morning, I had a new patient come into the office with shoulder and low back pain. She was a young lady with three children and related her pain to picking up kids and having babies. I was surprised when I looked at her case history and saw that she was only twenty-one and already had three children, one of whom was six. I wondered how she faired having children at such a young age, wondered if getting pregnant at fourteen was difficult. High school must have been tough sometimes—having to miss certain parts of being a teen because she was busy being a young mom. But her answers to my questions really surprised me. She told me she had missed all the dances and football games, all the parties and graduations and such, and when I questioned her about what she thought about that, her answer was profound. She simply said, **"When I found out I was pregnant, I just decided to change the way I thought about my life."** She went on to say, **"And I've had a wonderful experience with my children ever since. It's been great being a mom, I love it!"**

Think about it, consider all the places this young mom could have gone in her mind with that pregnancy, and look at what she chose, look at the quality of experience she decided to create. What a strong Power Statement for a young mother and father to make, because he did the same thing. And over the years, they became absolutely happy parents of three children beautiful children. What an expression of free will, of personal strength, what an expression of self-love, coming from such a young person. Needless to say, I was impressed. She didn't beat herself up for her mistakes—didn't ever choose to see them as mistakes. She just looked at her life and saw what she needed to do, and she continued her unfolding journey as a young parent. It changed a lot of things in all directions for her, and she decided to enjoy the direction that was now her life. As I've said many times before, there's no point in making yourself miserable over things you have no control over. There's a huge Power Statement to be had when we finally step back and simply allow life to present itself, and we find the space to look deeper at what it's offering rather than resisting it.

Finding the Power Statement

Finding our Power Statements is discovering the words and actions that impact our heart and inspire our lives. It's largely about exploring quality of thought, because it's our thinking that most impacts our experience and, subsequently, how we interact with life. It's through thought that we choose to expand into or away from our heart. Our Power Statements help us define and keep on track with that.

So can we step back from all our busyness and accomplishments long enough to understand that whatever we hold precious in our mind is responsible for our experience in this life? It's the quality of our thought that drives the anxiety we feel. It's thought that fosters how we care for a world that was made to support us. And it's thought that's the primary factor contributing to our spiritual and emotional evolution.

Our selfish ideas, our desires, and our careless, unrestrained thinking creates only more of the same. Abuse of ourselves, others, or this planet directly impacts our next move and continued action in this world unless we find the integrity within ourselves to do an about-face on the quality of our thinking. A single thought held by a society at large can impact generations of this world to come for thousands of years. The thoughts we hold—that feed our actions—do, indeed, impact the very quality of life on this planet.

On a more personal level, our pain, our anguish, and anxiety are all based in the quality of our thinking—in their cultivation as well as their resolution. It's the quality of our thinking that directs the perception of

our feelings. We see those feelings through the lens we choose; a lens of denial or as a victim, or we see them as lessons, even gifts, and on a bad day, we might see them through fear or as a nuisance.

It's our perception that drives our experience and directs our healthy or unhealthy interaction with life. It's a choice to make life a stronger, more courageous experience by answering the questions of how to re-organize and heal our thinking; how to choose to create an internal environment that helps us heal ourselves and and walk forward toward healing the world around us. Because how will we save ourselves, much less the Earth, if not through the quality of our thinking—the very thinking that motivates, coordinates, and inspires our actions?

This leads me right into my favorite Power Statement:
The choices that we make determine the lives that we live.
To thine own self be true.

Power Statements:
Defining and Dictating Your Inner Stance

As you're exploring your Power Statements, you'll find ones that really resonate with you. Ask yourself questions about them:

- Why do I like this?
- What is the deeper meaning in it for me?
- Does it help me explore aspects of my life in new and different ways?
- Is there any part of this that's more a trick of the mind to keep me thinking in old patterns that don't work, or is it a true Power Statement for me?
- How does this Power Statement help to strengthen my personal inner stance?

A Power Statement is inherently a tool of building life; a lever used to help you define the inner stance that you'd like to walk through life with. When you allow it, it helps maintain you in the direction of your deeper, heart-centered choices. There is no Power Statement that encourages fear or any of the children of fear, like greed, anxiety, resentment, or regret. A Power Statement will not encourage greed, it will not encourage revenge, it will not encourage violence or gossip. The Power Statement only encourages an internal statement that defines the integrity of our heart.

Power Statements should:
- resonate with your heart.
- integrate with the highest qualities of who you are and what you wish to learn.
- never maintain you in directions of dysfunction.
- help create, build, and rediscover your personal strength, wisdom, compassion, and love.
- create breath, and enhance your ability to breathe into life.
- never deplete you or anyone around you.

What a Power Statement Is and What It Is Not!

A Power Statement is a healing statement you can present to your heart, a statement of rejuvenation for the soul.

Think of your Power Statements as healing statements—a sort of proclamation that helps you grow and heal your heart and mind. Through them, we can help heal the toxic emotions, negativity, and pain that binds us. They help us create a salve to soothe the struggles that so poignantly tear at your heart, healing all the confusion, traumas, and "What the hell?" feelings of this human condition we're all trying to work our way through and make sense of.

Sometimes all it takes to create a Power Statement is one little word of love. Gratitude is a good start. It can be an answer to the poison, toxicity, and stress we all give far too much of our attention to. There are many more to explore: kindness, humility, caring, compassion, even welcome, or allowing ourselves to have great strength. Your job is to find what speaks to you today.

What a Power Statement Is Not

It's just as important to define what a power statement is not. It is not a show of arrogance or overt strength, but it is strength of character. Power Statements don't create fear, violence, and anxiety or any of the characteristics of a mind with unkempt emotional boundaries. It's not about greed, power, or how much money you can make, but it is about cultivating the ability to be content and to see the abundance of this world. It's not about how strong you are or how much better you are than somebody else. It's not based in the ego or based in the need to show off or be right. But it is about healthy and kind behavior towards others. Our greatest power is based in self-love, not self-adoration.

I have a friend who is a priest. And he figures that everybody deserves twenty minutes of his time no matter who they are or what is going on with them. That is how he begins every interaction, with kindness and generosity of time. That is his Power Statement, for himself and to the world. He chooses to see everyone as worthy, and his attention to them lets them know that. No one above, no one below. He chooses to give them the dignity of his time, no matter what. And by honoring everyone, he honors himself.

ROSCOE

Power Statements are never disrespectful of anyone, including ourselves.

Power Statement Do's and Dont's

Yup, Power Statements never destroy, and always build and support our journey.

- Power Statements are healthy and revitalizing for the heart, they're never depleting.
- Our Power Statements don't give us blind permission to get stuck in our negative thinking. They don't give us permission to get stuck anywhere—only to move and expand. Getting stuck is the result of our choosing a quality of thought that does not connect us with our heart, rather we chose a quality of thinking that separates us from the deeper truth of who we are. In the end, it tends to result in drama, negative thought, anxiety and fear, not our objective.
- A Power Statement never asks us or gives us permission to wish harm on anyone. How counterproductive would that be?
- A Power Statement doesn't make our fear-based judgment acceptable. It doesn't want you to stay stuck in your fearful and negative beliefs about others, and it doesn't encourage you towards hate or bad feelings of any kind. Power Statements simply encourage the strongest and healthiest quality of respect, honor, integrity, and all the qualities of love that you can cultivate and use to walk through this world with.
- A Power Statement won't let you take anything others do or say

personally. It doesn't encourage holding on to hurt feelings of any kind. But it does ask you to learn to see the world with eyes of strength, understanding, compassion, and kindness.

- A Power Statement won't ever encourage you to commit acts of violence, however, it will encourage you to stand up for yourself and those too weak to protect themselves. Yes, there's absolutely a difference.

- Power Statements never cultivate fear, violence, low self-worth, less-than feelings, or prolonged shame in anyone, ever.

- Power Statements won't let you feel like you're above or below anyone.

- And Power Statements won't condone anything that's depleting to the heart or counterproductive to our journey.

How-To Power Statements

Create the habit of forming questions for yourself; questions that give you some good direction on where you need to look, what you need to work on for your Power Statements. For example, if you think kindness is an issue, honestly ask, *Am I kind enough?* Then explore that. Explore what it is for you to be and express kindness from the heart. Do the same for courage, compassion, personal power, open-mindedness, and healthy judgment. Through life, when you're confronted with concepts of growth, ask yourself how you can explore and expand through them in the healthiest ways.

- Do you feel like you need to explore a little bit more compassion in your life?
- Do you feel like you need to explore a little bit more understanding in your life?
- Do you feel like you need to explore a little bit more courage in your life?
- Do you feel like you need to explore a little bit more rational thinking in your life?
- Do you feel like you need to explore a little bit more relaxation in your life?
- Do you feel like you need to explore a little bit more love in your life?
- Do you feel like you need to explore a little bit more healthy parenting in your life?
- Do you feel like you need to explore a little bit more healthy leadership in your life?
- Do you feel like you need to explore a little bit more healthy behavior in your life?
- And so forth…

Personal Example:

I've always struggled with what to do with people in need, particularly people asking for handouts. *What should I do? Are they being honest or manipulative?*

Power Statement for where I might like to improve myself: **It's okay for me to help those obviously in need.**

So I ask myself:
- Do I feel like I need to explore what it is to be a little kinder to others in my life?
- Do I feel like I need to explore what it is to be a little more generous with the time and money in my life?

Back to our kindness example:

Regarding kindness in your life, Mother Teresa might have some answers. You'll find yourself smiling at people and talking to people without so much hesitation if you study this woman just a little bit through her quotes.

Check out these quotes from Mother Teresa and try to find a Power Statement for yourself that you can relate to:

"Not all of us can do great things. But we can do small things with great love."

"Kind words can be short and easy to speak, but their echoes are truly endless."

"If you can't feed a hundred people, then feed just one."

"We shall never know the good that a simple smile can do."

"The most terrible poverty is loneliness, and the feeling of being unloved."

"If you judge people, you have no time to love them."

ROSCOE

Some of my personal favorites, my go-to quotes when I'm feeling unkind, taken advantage of, or judgmental, are:

> "Intense love does not measure, it just gives."
> -Mother Teresa

> "Be kind, for everyone you meet is fighting a fierce battle."
> -Philo of Alexandria

> "There are no human enemies, there are just people in pain asking for help."
> -Sylvia Boorstein

These quotes can help me find my power, help me touch my kindness, compassion, and understanding in place of a confused, frustrated, or angry mind.

> *I always find it incredibly interesting to research quotes from various writers and speakers. I think it's because when we find someone who thinks, someone who really embraces this journey of being human, we find that their unique way of expressing the concepts of life are really quite common to all of us. They seem to explore and share the knowledge that we all need in order to uncover our own facets of love in this life. They begin to unfold the wisdom and the secrets of the heart that we're also searching for. All we have to do is open to their words.*

Power Statements Rely on Our Quality of Thought

There's power in our great capacity to think and then make choices about the quality of that thinking. And it's through that gift that we reflect either the power of love or the fear we deplete ourselves with into our lives. Choices of thought and the quality of that thought reflect our choices everywhere, they impact all our lifestyle choices as well—choices in diet, our interaction and communication with each other, it motivates the actions we take in every day living, what exercise we choose to do or not to do, and the general tone of how we overall move through our lives.

> *"And the day came when the risk to remain tight in a bud was more painful than the risk it took to blossom."*
> –Anais Nin

Our Everyday Conversation Power Statements

Pay attention to life as it moves through and past you. Of course there are concepts of weakness and fear that we hear, but when you're listening, there are concepts of power that we hear in everyday conversation as well—nuggets of wisdom that fall in our laps, perhaps as a result of a simple chat with friends, family, or some private discussion at work. We might even be graced with some wisdom from that occasional stranger (that angel) who touches our heart or somehow guides us for a split second. Regardless of where it comes from, take note. Write your moment down, regarding what was said so you can reconnect with it, explore it

later for more understanding. Dictate a little story to yourself on your phone, or jot down the important words on a napkin. Just find a place to put the memory so you can recall the essence of what happened or what was said.

A Power Statement Around Diet

It's simple, and sometimes not-so-simple, making choices that reflect what's healthiest for yourself. But be assured, as long as the choice is based in creating health, what you do and how you do it is secondary. Do what works best for you in your current understanding of what's healthy, avoiding what's unhealthy. Don't sweat it too much because as your understanding of health changes, so will your choices. Once you decide to get on that gravy train (yes, a rather ironic choice of words), once you get on the train of getting healthy, you'll find new doors will naturally open—ones that you never imagine existed. And still, your choices are all based on doing what works best for you. The power of diet comes from paying attention to and knowing what's working and what's absolutely not. And herein, the choices that you make will dictate the body, mind, and life that you'll help create.

A Power Statement Around Exercise

The diet scenario is also true for exercise. It's a simple choice of finding your best quality of movement for the individual benefit of you. Discovering the quality of movement that best facilitates strength, health, and a positive state of wellbeing. This is your personal Power Statement to work on. It's the one that helps you nurture your physical form. You'll explore many avenues of all kinds of things, including exercise, diet, religion, politics, friends, and lifestyles. And whatever you're doing in the moment is your choice, until you find a stronger way of being. But until then, it's your best choice right now. All we have are choices that are right for now until we can choose better. So maintain your intention on what helps you expand, what allows you to grow, love, and know yourself better. And embrace a life that allows you to thrive in the healthiest of ways, now.

Look for the Power Statement Idioms Passed Down Through the Ages

There's a reason we've historically come up with idioms like, "Don't give it a second thought," or, "Don't overthink it." These two were built on getting caught up in our contemplative thinking, and compulsively mulling over things, so we make up a phrases that helps us sidestep that. We find or create a Power Statement reset that can help us reboot our challenged mind.

Historically, we've come up with many phrases that help us reformat our thinking around the confusion, anxiety, and perplexity that comes with being human. Obviously, we've always had our struggles and challenges in this human journey.

I love the Latin phrase, "Carpe diem." It helps remind me to be here now. When someone says, "Carpe diem," it's an idiom that means, "Seize the day." It helps us create an intention to take charge of the day, to live in the present moment, and not worry about the future.

Examples of common idioms:
- Cross that bridge when you come to it.
- Don't cut off your nose to spite your face.
- Oh, don't even go there.
- Don't get me started.
- Don't get your bowels in an uproar!
- Don't give it another thought.
- Don't think twice about it.
- Don't have a cow!
- Don't hold your breath.
- Don't judge a book by its cover.
- Don't poop where you eat.
- The ball is in your court.
- Don't bite off more than you can chew.
- It's a blessing in disguise.
- Don't count your chickens before they hatch.
- Don't put all your eggs in one basket.
- Every cloud has a silver lining.
- Straight from the horse's mouth.
- the whole nine yards

Taking Steps to Create Yourself

Below is an example of a personal Power Statement I recently came up with for me, myself, and I; a Power Statement for me to explore within myself! It's my personal statement on the subject of desire and the shortcomings of greed.

"I will not live my life in accumulation. I am here to live more,
to give more, to be more of what I am in this world.
This does not require gold, it requires courage. That is my gold."

Choosing your Power Statements is really about choosing your life, choosing the quality of thought you want to walk through this world with. It's about choosing what to do with your personal internal dialogue and the external expression of that dialogue. Choosing your Power Statement automatically asks you to maintain its message, allowing it to become more, and to expand within you. That expansion may not always feel comfortable, but it's always preferable to maintaining yourself in old patterns.

The Power Statements we select represent us claiming our power to choose our life —choosing what our life will look like, choosing how we will live it, and determining the thinking that drives our journey back to ourselves. It's a journey that requires us to say, "I am worth it!" And you are, so step forward and choose your most powerful life—one that moves through your heart and out into the world in the strongest of ways. This life is not for others to approve for you. It's for you to claim through your own heart. So claim it, and go create yourself.

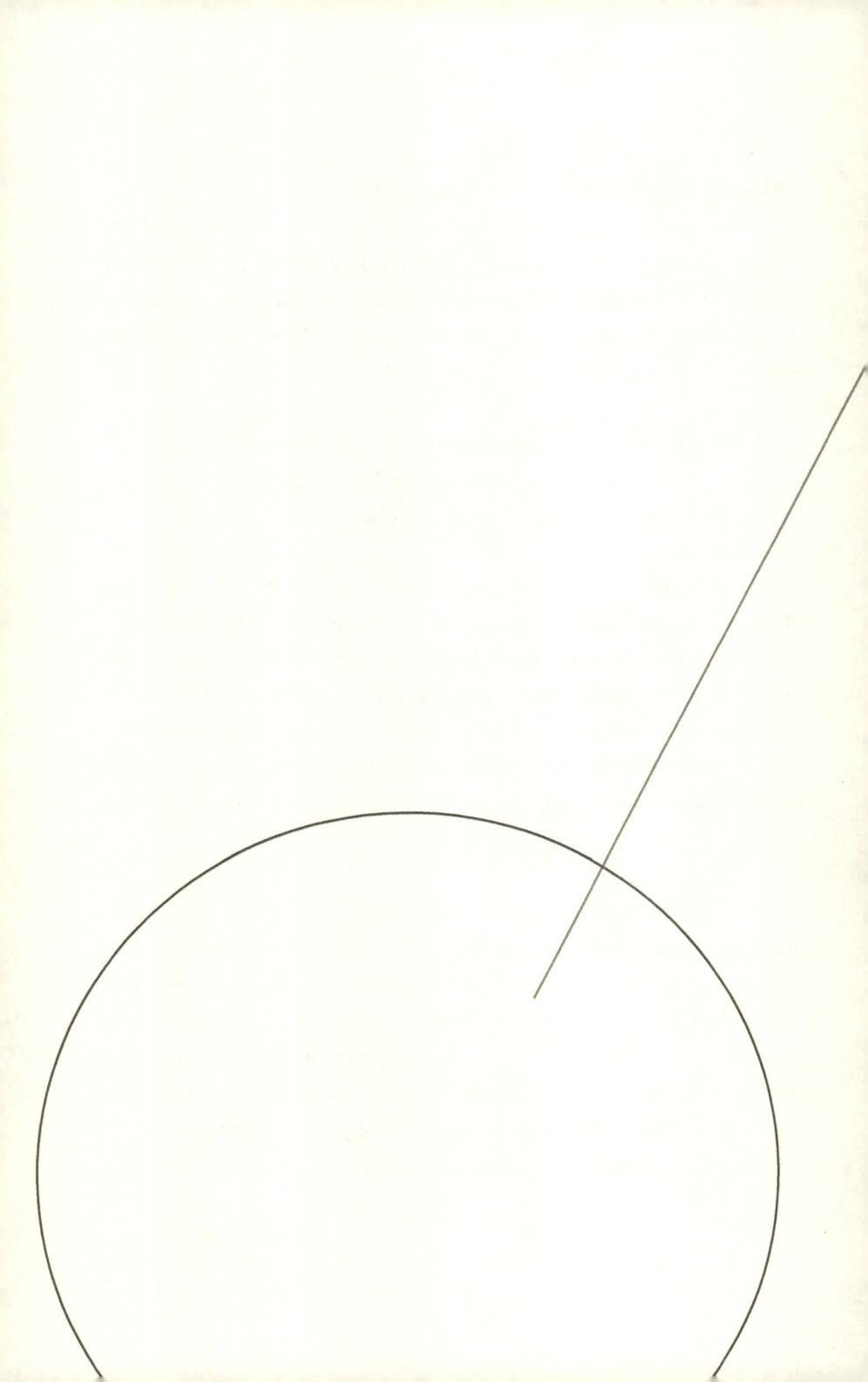

Part Three
Living Life as a Power Statement

Build-a-Power STATEMENT
get real and explore yourself

Here's your opportunity to begin that portion of your journey that helps keep you on track, maintain your direction, and helps reinforce what's most important to you. This is where you build your reminders and your re-connectors of life, the words and statements that help inspire you to become all the impressive things that you know you are but items that maybe you've lost track of along your way. This is where you learn how to make a project out of exploring for, finding, and building your very personal list of Power Statements.

First Step: Get Real!
Yeah, you heard me! Get real with yourself. It's your first, most important step in finding, recognizing, and owning your Power Statements. That means getting honest with your struggles, taking a good look at all the potential the work in front of you, and looking at all your naturally glitchy tendencies, knowing yourself, as well as looking at what's really, really important to your heart. So, eyes and mind open! Everyone has

their strengths and their weaknesses, their life-inspired ideas, concepts and wisdom that drive them—all of them are inherent in the design of our beautiful human reality.

Explore yourself. Sometimes the toughest part is admitting it to ourselves what we fear most: failure, weakness, our own strength, being alone or not being enough in this world, a sense of inadequacy, the seduction of greed, or an overzealous ego. There's plenty of subject matter to choose from, after all, we're human, there are plenty of places for us to slip up, and plenty of inspiration, goodness and love to explore. This is your time to step it up, look in the mirror, and have a chat with yourself. We have good and bad habits that we've accumulated or inherited, interests and wisdom nuggets we've acquired, that all somehow influence our world. And it's up to us to identify them, look for the depleting or stagnating ones, and the ones we want to explore more. Then it's our job to find a productive way to move in them, to help the struggles shift so they no longer weigh us down so heavily and help the wisdom expand.

So, get to work. If you haven't done it already, make a list of all the places that you can work on and expand into in your world. Explore your weaknesses, your struggles, your strength, your addictive ways, and your disruptive quality of thinking as well as your inspired ways. The question is always: *How can you move into what feeds your heart and out of the ideas that just don't suit it?* Make a list. Take note of everything that can be worked with to build your wellbeing.

Next Step

After you've identified some of the powerful concepts that you want to work with, find those glitches and those ideas of the heart you so need to work on. And when you recognize their importance to your journey, how depleting and toxic they can be, as well as their potential for healing, try and find general categories for them. Where do these things fit in your mind? A glitch can be anything from the judgments you throw around at the people you care about most, to your cynicism and the negative thoughts you have about the world at large.

Now I've had my life's share of being judgmental or feeling judged (neither one is particularly enjoyable). I've found myself stuck in different types of racial fears generated by my own ignorance, usually due to my own inexperience. I've been perplexed by the religious confusion that seems to abound in most faiths, questioning, *Is anybody right? Is anybody wrong?* I don't know, but if you don't watch it, it seems to create a lot of space where fear, negativity and judgment can enter.

I've spent lifetimes losing myself to greed, self-centered interests or desires, being grouchy, angry, resentful, insecure, not feeling enough, feeling victimized, feeling above, and acting downright stupid. And yes, the list goes on! There's plenty to work on, plenty of positive exploration to apply to any depleting quality you might own. There's work to do and the lessons to be had. And yes, this is the work of life—this is the journey of self awareness.

The truth of it is that when judgment and negativity happens, it most profoundly damages the one who's doing the judging, the one stuck

in the negativity. So look for your own glitches so you can do the work of the heart and take down those emotional charges a peg.

And exploring the truths you already hold dear, the wisdom you've already touched within your heart and your mind only needs to be continued, to be reinforced and expanded. That can be as simple as doing your research on words of the heart, as we mentioned earlier, or recognizing traits of the heroes we want to emulate. For example: Gandhi and his capacity for compassion, Fred Rodgers and his ability to see the best in others, Steve Jobs and the courage he showed and shared for his life's journey.

Last Step

Get real, identify, and finally **explore, explore, explore** the words, quotes, and ideas about healing any and all the parts of your body, mind, and spirit—the you that only wants to know wellbeing.

> *Note:* Have patience with the process. Recognition of what needs work and all the wisdoms that you value will unfold in its appropriate time. If your journey is anything like mine, you'll start looking for one word or idea, and suddenly three other concepts will be staring you in the face, just waiting for your exploration. So take a note, write them down so you can refer back when the time is right.

Patience with the Process: Your Beginning and Your Continuing Journey of Courage

Question what's most vital to you, what's deeply important in your life. Have you ever looked at the qualities of being alive and awake that you really, really, really need to work on most? What are they? Have you tried to explore the deepest questions living in your heart as you move through this world of yours? Have you spent time evaluating the biggest and most profound gifts of being alive and present to this unfolding life you're part of? Have you given careful thought to this journey, given deep consideration to what holds the very most light for us all? If not now, when? Opening to these questions, even a little bit, gives them permission to evolve through us. Give yourself permission to begin.

In exploring yourself in a deeper way, you're expressing a profound dedication to being alive to your world and validating your desire to thrive in it. And to truly thrive requires a presence to the abundance and miracles held in life. This requires the patience to change. It's a big and real patience for us as we come to the understanding that what we often believe in one moment may not necessarily be true for us in the next. What's most or least important for us from day to day can be a slippery, temporary idea that will, indeed, change. It has to as it evolves through you.

So, as you move forward towards all your new moments, it's best not to get too firmly attached to any one concept or idea. This is where "patience with our process of becoming" comes in. Patience with the ideas we attach to, with the experiences we find ourselves embroiled in,

and patience with everything human that can seem confusing and disorienting to the heart. Because it's with patience that we give ourselves the freedom to ask the questions in life that really matter, and with patience that we might receive our answers.

That's all pretty big stuff. Take a minute and just meditate on that for a bit before you move forward to the next paragraph.

In a nutshell, be patient with your evolutionary process, because things are going to change, and part of change is, indeed, your patience and everything it touches.

> *"Wonder is the beginning of wisdom."*
> –Socrates

New Roads, New Life

As we expand and evolve, we'll naturally find ourselves re-negotiating how we want to live. We'll find ourselves looking down roads that we never even knew existed—alive roads and paths of the heart—catching those spontaneous rides that help us reflect on the biggest parts of who we are. Our job is to integrate ourselves into all those new ideas we've come across, and to move past what we were, and know that because of all this, we've grown. In all the confusion of this work, we'll naturally wonder how the heck we ended up in this new place of the heart, this life of more truth.

But when we think about it, we'll realize how we got here—we know our life's nothing less than the best, most beautiful adventure into our precious world, that nothing happens without a deep connection to one who only wants for our good, and that there's an impossible-to-know purpose in everything. And at worst, it's a wild and crazy ride, structured to reach the same final destination if we only we were to breathe a little and let it be.

This journey always brings lessons. Make a list of yours. Where are your biggest lessons? How and why do they exist? What allowed you to find them, how do you know they're there? Look back at the biggest, most irritating, exciting, dramatic, difficult, or fun lessons and realizations of your life, recall all that you learned through those experiences, and put them on your list. They might be the repeating stories in your life, and they're surely the difficult or most heart-wrenching experiences of your life. Your lessons might even come through the irritating itches that you try to ignore, the ones that just won't leave you alone. But no matter what has caught your attention or made you think and reflect on your world, take a note, make a list. Theres a gift there somewhere, a life lesson to be learned, big or small, waiting.

Note: **Recognize resistance.** Lessons come in all forms, so pay attention to what you're trying to dodge and avoid. What we're most resistant to is often what we should be paying attention to, even though we want to look elsewhere. It's where the big work hides. So, keep your eyes and heart open, stay alert to yourself. It's the difficult ideas and the painful personal concepts that can hold the greatest gifts on this journey.

Power Statement Sharing Hints

As you talk about your statements and your journey, always keep in mind that others see, hear, and experience life in their own unique way; that your personal favorite Power Statement will be seen differently by others than by you, because perceptions are based in the unique life experience and background of the individual. The impact of your Power Statement touches them distinctively, sometimes in a very different way than it may have touched you. You can learn from that, especially if you're willing to listen to the perspective of others, either through clarification of your own experience, or simply through understanding that we are all rather peculiar in our own ways and see life through a lens that is born only through us. All of our Power Statements and words hold a meaning unique to the individual, meanings that are personally ours, that move through your precious individual heart.

My point is simple but sometimes overlooked. Sharing your Power Statements and the impact they have on you is a wonderful thing to do with others, but it's inadvisable to expect others to resonate exactly as you do regarding any particular Power Statement. So watch yourself. When you have something to share, let it inspire others in whatever way it's meant to. Don't ever expect anyone to respond to life exactly as you do. It's a simple rule for sharing Power Statements and it makes it more fun and interesting. When we open to the ideas beyond the clarity of our own meaning about something, we naturally find new and fresh understanding that benefits us, so be sure to listen.

Keep Your Ear to the Ground

Keep your ears, your eyes, and your mind open and awake! When you hear words you don't understand, jot them down. If your mind catches a phrase or quote that intrigues it, stop and figure out where it came from. Don't just let it slip by. If you think you're going to remember it but have some things to do, it's ill-advised to not make a note that you can come back to later. Chances are, it'll become a lost memory. The same is true for ideas, and proposed actions of any kind, or concepts that you want to embrace. Take note! Don't let them scatter to the winds of a busy life.

I remember during meditation class with Sylvia Boorstein, she was explaining how she was intrigued by the word "ineffable." She let everyone know she was enjoying exploring it. I was intrigued, so I wrote it down, I did my research, because I wasn't familiar with it either, and found out it's an awesome concept. Now it's a strong part of my vocabulary, a huge word that helps me interact with ideas of the heart on a higher level than before. "Ineffable" is a word that helps me reconnect with the understanding that we are infinite, so I use it. It works for me.

Go find your words, the ones that work for you and your heart. Hunt down the words that help you reconnect with your deep truth. They're worth tracking down for the journey. I guarantee it!

Ineffable: *too great or extreme to be expressed or described in words.*

Journey Work is Ageless

As you explore, don't worry about age. Curiosity knows no time of life. It exists in every phase from childhood to the curiosity we have before we die. So, don't worry about age, just worry about embracing life, about your journey work—the work of the spiritual warrior.

The work of the heart is ageless.

You can begin at any time. You can learn and grow right up until you take your last breath. So never hesitate because you believe you're too old, and never ever give up the search for wisdom, truth, and love within.

A Powerful Reminder

I wrote this poem for my daughter, Lauren. It was meant as a Power Statement from me to her, so that she might remember her own wonder—a wonder she was born with, like all of us. My daughter's wonder is the same wonder imparted to everyone. It's an internal wonder and it never leaves us. So, really, this was written for everyone; written for all the sons and daughters, all the mothers and fathers and grandparents of the world. We can all find ourselves struggling to remember our truth, yearning to reconnect with our heart in this world. So this poem, *Lauren's Poem*, is written to remind us of our origins, and to help us uncover our pure and human connection that we all have with life.

POWER STATEMENT LOGBOOK

I am lovable
I am valuable
I make a difference
I am enough
I am worthy
I belong

Can you whisper these six simple lines to yourself without reservation? Can you hold them in your heart, knowing their message already exists in you? This gentle poetry is for your personal remembering, and yet its message is meant for everyone.

I am lovable, I am valuable, I make a difference
I am enough, I am worthy, I belong.

These are the words we're meant to speak to ourselves, to own their truth with a conviction that spans the distance beyond our self-judgment, pain, and fear. This is your gift to you, and it frees you to share yourself with the world.

A flower needs no help to be what it's meant to be.
It can exist and blossom in the most difficult environments,
and you are no different.

Often, our most personal growth requires removing the blockages to our awareness of what love can accomplish when we open to it. And that begs the question: can you open your heart to love like a flower opens itself to the sky?

*So be grateful for the flowers,
they bring color, brilliance, and grace to the world,
and you do exactly the same.*

Remember, this world is yours to share your heart with, to expand yourself into, and learn through. So open yourself to its gifts, open to love and growth, and to the wisdom of the heart. Open up, let yourself take root in this place and blossom.

Big Reboot

There are sinkholes of the mind that we all periodically fall into.

Irrational thinking, general overwhelm, and frustration around the sheer busyness and complication of living in this world are a few sinkholes. We all have common glitches that we encounter which need to be renegotiated and rebooted so we can re-connect with our center. The whole point of my writing, of Power Statements, and maintaining quality of thought, is to help us reconnect with what it is to live through our heart and not at the mercy of our thinking minds. Once we've recognized that we're off course, that's where exploring for Power Statements begins—finding a statement that helps you reboot back to yourself.

From this point, develop your criteria for Power Statements as they relate to the most common emotional struggles. For example, contemplation and micromanagement: Describe how these can relate to life, how they can create disruption, and find ways to explore so that you might find your perfect Power Statement—one that helps you re-negotiate those emotions encouraging you to find healthier ways to move forward in life.

- What helps you re-connect with stable, rational thinking when you've found a sinkhole?
- Where and how do you recalibrate around the hole?
- What have been your most productive tools to move you forward, and how long does it usually take to move?
- Do you have a favorite author, speaker, quote, word, story, quality of exercise, breath, internal stance, place to meditate from that historically helps brings you around?
- Are there any people or tools that you've always wanted to look at? And would now be a good time?

Perfectionism Reboot

Sometimes we need a Power Statement to balance the irrational idea that we need to be perfect. It's a common "glitch in the matrix!" When you notice it, take a minute and search for your personal antidote. Maybe search for others who have struggled with the same negative concepts, the perfectionism, and the lie of not being enough. It can help when you can find a potential "teacher" who has identified similar personal challenges and hopefully found a positive way to address them. If you find something good, if your antidote comes up, grab onto it, even if it's only a close second. It's a beginning, and if it works, write it down.

You are amazing. You always have been.
Any ideas to the contrary are simply wrong.

What are the words, phrases, and exercises that allow you to accept yourself as you are right now, to honor your existence and help you move through life with a quality of self-love and self-respect that is unshakable and strong?

Finding Power

The wisdom that we need to move through life with is generally not taught by society or even by our parents. That's because they don't own it, and they haven't done their due diligence to find it. The truth is, they can only teach what they have. And if you've lived your life in the lie, you think the lie is the truth, and that's what you teach.

"There are no great limits to growth because there are no limits of human intelligence, imagination, and wonder."
-Ronald Reagan

We all learned at an earlier time to be less than we actually are, asked by someone or something to be small in a world we were meant to be vast in. Perhaps we were taught by our parents, family, or friends, because they themselves were influenced by a society that squelched the human spirit, and they learned to be that way through their family and friends. Regardless of how we got there, we were asked to become less than what we were so that others would not feel so insecure or alone in this world. The concept that "misery loves company" was very real to them, even if they didn't know it, and the children, students, and employees that were created were destined to live in a way that made sure nobody felt uncomfortable, that everyone rose to their highest level of surviving without stepping on fragile egos. We were all taught very well how to not make waves, and if we needed to, to make them in such a way that they could be controlled by another.

This unwanted legacy gets ended through your Power Statements. Within that, we can all begin again by embracing new qualities of thinking that are free from fear, free from the opinions of others, and that allow us to live as we were meant, knowing the strength of a life with meaning—our own meaning, and all that we were meant to become.

Aaron's Affirmation

I have a stepson of sorts who struggles with staying out of trouble. His journey is one of learning a deeper part of who he is and allowing that to be his internal compass. One day Aaron was in the office doing

work with me on exactly that topic. The topic of emotional transformation. Changing himself in a way where his old patterns of behavior were given the opportunity to fade away. This is what he said to me. He had the words down perfectly, "I am willing to re-wire how I conduct myself, based on who I want to be rather than who I was taught to be." He went on, "Irrational behavior and aggression are not ways to exist in life and empower myself. They do not belong to my truth. They are not part of my essence. They are learned behaviors that have never helped me express who I am." And this was his Power Statement—what he used to guide himself.

We must teach each other the power of our own essence, and we can't do that until we teach ourselves. It's not always easy, but it's always worth it. You just can't mind that it's difficult.

Avoid Negative Power Statements. Because they're not really Power Statements. They're covert statements of depletion disguised by the mind to make you feel as though you're strong. So, be alert. The truth is you don't need them in your life.

Fear has a purpose, but we abuse it. We use it for things that don't require fear. And then healthy fear becomes an unnecessary and a maladaptive kind of fear that creates an adrenaline reaction in an environment that doesn't require adrenaline. It actually might only require listening and understanding. So our distracted reaction leaves us depleted and confused about who we are because we've misused this tool of fear that was given to us for real survival, not to maintain us in our disfunction. This kind of fear will not facilitate our heart-centered communication. Fear is not meant for our daily interaction with one another. Fear, used properly, helps us move through life safely. Aside from that, it can be quite disruptive when we use it as a primary guide in our journey.

So pay attention to your words and your Power Statements. Sometimes, phrases like, "Keep your friends close, and your enemies closer," don't really serve a purpose unless said in fear. Ask yourself, do you really want to walk around with that in the back of your mind, or as your primary guide?

Power Statements for When Physical Symptoms Provide You Indicator Lights

When you find yourself clenching your teeth, furrowing your brow, scaring little children without even trying, well, perhaps your mind is entertaining life in a way unfamiliar or incongruent with your heart. It's a tough state of mind. You notice you're walking through life and you haven't seen a thing, haven't stopped, not even in your mind, to appreciate even one moment in getting to your destination. Basically, you step back and realize that you've missed the whole trip. So with a furrowed brow, grinding teeth, and an aggression in your step, breath, and mannerisms, with a quality of speech that seems too abrupt for who you know you are, you step back and quizzically look at yourself. Your self-awareness is putting you on notice that you're living in a way that isn't true to you—you're missing your life. It's a moment of gold for the heart, this internal reflection grabbing at you and trying to tell you that you need to stop and listen; that it's time to re-coordinate with your truth, to hear the beat of your own heart again.

When you find yourself stuck in an internal place that doesn't suit your truth, remember: All these feelings, all these distractions and disruptions, they're all part of the human experience, and we all find ourselves immersed in some version of them at some point in life. And when we recognize we're stuck somewhere, it's our job to keep track of it, and to re-evaluate the tone of how we're walking through life with negativity. We're being asked to open ourselves up to finding that internal nature that suits our truth and our life-walk far better. When we can renegotiate that attitude, when we reboot and get back to something of our truth, we can breathe again, and we can relax our jaw a bit, because we've entered a place that's far more familiar to our heart. There's greater ease for us here, a deeper connection to what's real for us, an ability to see something other than our tension and anxiety. It's a stark comparison for us when we find ourselves in a place that doesn't suit us at all versus the relief that we get when we can relax into who we are.

Referring back to a position of strength and love, a Power Statement, a well designed breath, can help us reposition ourselves instantly back into our higher journey.

Power Statement Moving into Life

Making your choices from a place of strength rather than a place of fear allows life to unfold through that strength rather than absent of it.

In talking to a younger female patient about her relationship with her mother, she spoke with me about the dysfunction they have between them, the strained communication, tense atmosphere, and all the seemingly negative interaction. When she went home for the weekend, she took a definite leap of courage and addressed the situation personally with her mother. To her relief, her mother responded well. She said it gave her things to think about and that she would try to communicate and interact in a kinder, more understanding way.

Opening to new thought is an expression of love that doesn't always come easily, but when we do, it comes with gifts—gifts that we may never have had the opportunity to look at without a little human push from someone in pain. One of the morals of the story is it doesn't matter how old you are, whether you're a mother, father, daughter, or son, even if you're a great grandparent, you're always growing up. It's a good thing to embrace.

Secondary Power Statements That Influence Your Wellbeing

A Power Statement may not always be acquired through words, quotes, or phrases. They can be Power Statements of action, showing a belief in one's strength, truth or abilities, an activity, even a hobby that helps us unfold into self-loving choices. So move out! Give yourself permission to live your Power Statements. Let your actions and choices of personal power speak for themselves. Why not approach life as one big Power Statement to be alive to, to be an adventure in the best of ways?

Living our Power Statements isn't just our diet, our choice to exercise, be active, as well as rest, meditate, walk in the woods, our entertainment choices, vocations and choices in education, our hobbies and leisure time, to choose health over sickness (yes, we can do that), or to strive for resilience and a state of wellbeing that supersedes our problems. Aren't they all forms of Power Statements? Our Power Statements have the powerful ability to impact the life we're creating for ourselves in a wonderful way. The only question that accompanies that is: *will we let them?*

In a way, our Power Statements are like voting. And we vote with our forks, our purchases, our activities, our thinking, we vote through what we believe is important and worth our time, and the belief systems we hold to be true in our minds. We vote through all our choices in every aspect of our lives. And all these things add up to a quality of existence that determines how we see and experience life.

So why would we knowingly choose anything that's depleting over the choices in life that are enhancing? The warrior wants to remember and embrace the spark of life, the warrior wants to hold that spark close to themselves and to taste and have gratitude for all the moments of joy and the treasures of life. It's our job not to lose touch with that yearning.

Your Tribe of Choice
is a POWER STATEMENT
explore community and thrive

Our tribe, the community we most move and thrive with, can profoundly influence our journey into our hearts. They touch us, we touch them, and, in some ineffable way, we become one with the tribe we choose.

A Baseline for Tribe

A tribe should be empowering, offering us freedom to be and expand. They're the people we're trying to catch a glimpse of our own light through, and the ones we help to see their own. Ask yourself, *Do you grow through it, or stagnate with "your people?"*

Tribe should inspire groundedness, safety to expand, a breath of strength and comfort. It's us finding the people we can be ourselves with. Connecting with authentic, strong, supportive, and compassionate relationships. Having interactions with others that spur our growth, opens the heart, and inspires the mind.

In his book, *The Different Drum*, Scott Peck discusses the four stages of community formation. The fourth stage, he calls "true community," and it relates to the perspective of being connected to one's tribe.

Essentially, our most mature community (tribe) relies on our healthiest communication to thrive. The quality of being able to discuss life freely and without taking things personally—there exists a level of natural understanding where people are empathetic with each other and easily relate to one another's feelings. The tribe requires the cultivation of one's true self as an individual, and asks the same of others in order for the relationships to survive and thrive. Together, they acquire an unforced comfort, a safety, and a sense of understanding and presence with one another that surpasses the ego's temptation to be other than what they are. Acceptance is the inevitable result of being with your tribe, and any insecurities are simply part of our growth within ourselves, creating ripples of growth through the tribe.

In its healthiest form, our tribe encourages us become what's most important to us—it asks us to know ourselves. A tribe ideally leads us toward the best of what we can be and acts to help support our journey. A tribe holds us and inspires strength from us, and we do the same for our tribe.

As Dinah Maria Mulock Craik so beautifully put it:

"Oh, the comfort, the inexpressible comfort of feeling safe with a person; having neither to weigh thoughts nor measure words, but to pour them all out, just as they are, chaff and grain together, knowing that a faithful hand will take and sift them, keep what is worth keeping, and then, with a breath of kindness, blow the rest away."

True Tribes

Whether it's a big tribe or a one-person tribe, these are some of the qualities of a true tribe. And always remember that you are your most important tribe member! If you can't bring these qualities to yourself and others, receiving them might be questionable.

There's inspiration to be your best, most creative you through your tribe.
- Are you inspired to be your best, most creative you through your tribe, and do you do that for others?

The tribe feeds the hearts, souls, and minds of its members. No one is excluded.
- Does your tribe feed you, do you feed your tribe?

A tribe is felt in the heart.
- Is yours a tribe of the heart?

Knowing your tribe brings with it a high sense of belonging—belonging to a group as well as belonging in the world.
- Do the people you spend time with feed your sense of belonging in this world?

ROSCOE

Your tribe sees you, supports your unique and individual truth, while also adding to it.
- Does your tribe support your truth? Is there mutual growth and value exchanged?

A tribe is a natural place for good. It creates an open and safe environment for expression.
- And does your tribe offer you a comfort that is based in kindness as well as an ability to see past the difficulties of your life? Does it allow a safe place for the heart of who you are?

In your tribe, there's a sense of safe challenge, not always comfortable, but always empowering.
- Does your tribe support you and keep you in line when your choices are questionable or when old unhealthy patterns rear their dysfunctional heads?

Those who stand next to us will never intentionally force us to walk on eggshells. We're given safe-harbor to be ourselves in our own healthy way, and we will never be enabled in our unhealthy or self-destructive behavior.
- Does your world feel safe and free with those you spend your most valued time with? Do they give you permission to thrive in the healthiest of ways?

Moments of Tribal Recognition

We've all had moments of recognition from others—connection with people that "got" us. They were able to see who we were, and we just felt known. The memory might be faint, this essence of being seen. What was it like to be acknowledged, to feel like you belonged, even with one person? People come and go from our lives, moving through, and passing out of, this world. But they do impact us, and we feel forever touched when we feel seen, and we know through them what it is to be supported for the best of what we are.

Finding Tribe

Our tribe usually reflects our values, shares our yearning for growth, and encourages us to express ourselves authentically while simultaneously satisfying our need for a deeper human connection and knowledge that we belong. This is more than tends to be found in simple companionship.

Finding tribe may not always be easy, and it may not come quickly to us, but it can come in unexpected ways—with chance meetings and through people we previously didn't take much notice of. So you have to open yourself to the possibilities being presented, and allow life to flow through you. Allow for your mistakes and your effortless successes, and understand that your real tribe already exists within you. It's like everything else. It comes from within and expands outward. You simply offer yourself to those who cross your path with that same offer of an open heart. Because open hearts will always connect.

ROSCOE

> *"The bond that links your true family is not one of blood, but of respect and joy in each other's life. Rarely do members of one family grow up under the same roof."*
> -Richard David Bach

Suggestions for Finding Your Tribe in a Busy World

There are simply no guarantees that any club, organization, job, meet-and-match app on your phone, school, or church will guarantee that you'll find your heart-centered match. But tribe, on a deeper level, is that special group or individual who willingly journeys with you for a time, stands next to you as you grow.

Here are some suggestions of ways to explore for your tribe. Just remember to trust the intelligence that brings us together for what we need, often regardless of what our ego says.

Self-reflect.
The work of life is knowing yourself, and attracting your tribe requires a sense of yourself that goes beyond what society and your past has tried to lay on you. Spend time quietly getting to know your heart. Explore the concepts that touch your soul, looking at what's truly important rather than what you've been told is important by others. Understanding yourself allows you to invite others into your life in unexpected ways. So, courageously accept the invitation to expand.

Try new things.
Give yourself permission to explore and open to your areas of interest and things you're curious about. Allow that curiosity to unfold and to draw you forward. Similar hearts are attracted to similar endeavors. If you're drawn to the concepts of love, it's unlikely that organizations that reflect judgment will be on your radar.

Give yourself permission to re-evaluate.
Open yourself to the world in a fresh way.
When your heart tells you, give people that you may have previously put off a second chance. The truth may be that your prior impression may have been based in old judgment that no longer belongs to you or them. Never alienate a heart that needs your gentle affirmation. Finding your tribe may be more dependent on you opening your heart up and seeing the good in others than them seeing you first. And that's a journey by itself!

Listen to your heart if it whispers.
When you feel good and comfortable about something, nurture it a bit. If you don't, move forward, because our moments are all gifts easily lost. Sometimes we need to reach out, and if we listen, sometimes we need to back off. But listen, no matter what, because when you courageously stepped forward in life, no matter what, tomorrow can always be seen as another beautiful day of opportunity.

Put the word out.
If you know a type of people you want in your life, make it known! Here's where social media, friends, family, and groups you already hang

with can come in handy. There are people like you doing the same thing, looking for their tribe. No guarantee, but you might get lucky and recognize the essence of a tribe member, or they might recognize you. Just keep in mind: tribes and followers on social media are not necessarily the same thing.

Know what's most important!
Remember your heart, remember that you're lovable, remember that you make a wonderful difference here, have incredible value, remember that just being alive and you is enough, and remember that, without question, you belong in this world in a magnificent way. Stepping forward can be intimidating, but the world deserves to experience the worth that you bring. So step out, explore for your tribe, and touch people's hearts. Guaranteed, they're hungry for it. We all are.

    Our personal communities give us the opportunity for collaborative interaction with one another. They support the act of being pulled up by one another when we need it, and facilitate relationships that help us span the internal gap between feeling insecure and tired or strong and courageous. Whether it's one friend or the world, when we get sidetracked from our journey, our tribe helps us remember the love that pumps through us. So, in your search for community, hold close your heart. Remember, we're all part of the one tribe, and our greatest strength always lays in our prayers—not just prayers for one another, but with one another.

Life, Living as a Power Statement

Remember: Power Statements are not just words. They're movements, prayers, memories, experiences of living, and enlightened moments of the heart. They're postures, exercises, space alone, interactions with your tribe, taking someone you love out to coffee, or buying them a needed item.

Make a self-nurturing list:
- Things you can do to nurture yourself
- Things you can do to nurture others. Service always covertly nurtures the giver.

Yes, indeed, there's power in giving yourself permission to be pampered through receiving and giving. Because power statements are about claiming life for yourself, choosing to live the way your heart directs you no matter what you're being told by those around you. The wonderful thing about the heart is it always filters its choices through love. The same is true for Power Statements, and you just can't go wrong with that.

Deb's Power Statement
We Naturally Create Our Own Power Statements

An old friend of mine, Deb, called me one Sunday, very excited about an experience she'd had. She had her own perfect moment of inspiration, which she humorously referred to as, "My evangelical me."

ROSCOE

The previous night had been a sleepless night for Deb. She had been struggling with the imminent death of a friend, and found herself questioning found what she, Deb, was bringing into the world and leaving behind. What did Deb's legacy look like? And in a quiet moment, a thought of inspiration moved through her heart. The phrase Deb heard was, "Spread kindness and joy to everyone you meet and give thanks for every day." This became her personal Power Statement, meant for her, and potentially true for everyone. It came through her with a purpose, to help maintain the spark and soul of who she is, to keep her close to her heart.

An important point to note is, Deb was listening to the whisper within, and she allowed it to move through her freely. And her little gift from a higher state did not go unappreciated. She held it close and allowed it to guide her life. "Spread kindness and joy to everyone you meet and give thanks for every day," It's a statement that puts Deb back on track when she feels the struggle, attack, and vulnerability of life dragging her down. It's the statement that touches her heart and inspires a life that keeps her grounded in her tenderness and joy. This is Deb's personal declaration of love. It's her reminder of who she is.

Statements like this can come through any of us. We'll choose different words depending on who we are, but it's the essence of the words, the message behind them, that will draw us in toward our heart. Their message will always have a common underlying theme: remember love, remember your truth. It's how those words speak to our heart and the feelings that they cultivate within us that truly build a picture for us to live by. So find that perfect statement that works for you, that inspires you toward your love. Use Deb's if you want, or just explore until the words of your heart unfold for you.

Be Patient, Especially with Patience

Patience. This is a problem, an answer, and a Power Statement all in one word. It's a lesson we have to re-learn again and again, because patience and our ability to live a life reflecting it doesn't just happen all at once. It's more of a refinement within us, an accumulative experience with its expression living through us and cultivating its own special quality of presence.

Patience is one of those major lessons of life. Our growth in the world doesn't happen all at once, and we're not going to find every secret we need for enlightenment right away. It all takes time. We don't learn everything in one shot, nor should we assume to have the capacity to apply everything we learn immediately. We're human beings, not downloads in The Matrix, so have patience with the process. This life is a journey, not a destination. And it does, indeed, require a lifetime to reconnect with that which is infinite within us. That requires understanding and opening up to the wisdom of patience. So even when you find your perfect Power Statement for the day, and you write it somewhere—on the bathroom mirror or the back of your hand, you just jot it down anywhere—it still requires time for you to evolve into its meaning. You'll need time to let it change and transform within you, to move through you in all its forms.

ROSCOE

"Be patient. Patience is the mother of all virtues."
–Hrithik Roshan

*"You can't jump from little things to big things.
It just takes time and patience."*
–Nadia Comaneci

*"Tolerance, compromise, understanding, acceptance, patience -
I want those all to be very sharp tools in my shed."*
–CeeLo Green

All this patience stuff, it's all part of everyone's journey. Like all the roads to the best parts of yourself, it requires reminders and Power Statements of all kinds to rekindle those truths of the heart within you, to remind you of their presence and their importance. Like most virtues, patience must be earned through living it, and like all forms of love, it brings with it a grace of being that cannot be obtained without knowing and opening to its gift.

Walking a path of becoming ourselves requires our long-term commitment to being alive and present to life. It asks us all to lean towards and embrace this fantastic journey, committing ourselves in such a way that we're willing to change, transform, and find new approaches to walking in this world. We're asked to openly engage and explore for new understanding, always searching for stronger, more heart-centered and appropriate Power Statements to rely on as reminders of who and what we're becoming, and where we are now.

Take Time For Your Big Re-Read

Review your list of Power Statements periodically. It might even be helpful to create a schedule around it: once a day, once a week, once a month. Whatever works for you. It's powerful to revisit and immerse yourself in your entire list, in all the words of inspiration, the goals of the heart. It's a powerful experience to re-enter your journey, exploring the words and concepts that feed you.

How About Judgment?

Personally, I find myself quite vulnerable to judgment. Being judgmental about people, places, things, and ourselves is an equal opportunity employer of toxic and negative thinking. Sometimes it feels like I'm its favorite guy! My judgment is very open-minded, and it can go anywhere. It can be about someone I've had issues with—friend, family, or foe. It can be about judging myself. In my weak moments, I leave the door wide open and a little judgment even sneaks into the room with a simple glance at someone I don't even know, but my judgment sums some part of them up in a snap! Yeah, I'm usually dead wrong...

But I know that in holding onto judgment against anyone is akin to strangling my own heart; flipping the off switch and then wondering why it stopped beating. It reminds me of pushing a nail through my head while believing it'll make life more comfortable for me, that making someone else small makes me big. Yeah, it does something alright. It creates a nasty, suffering, stagnant, and unproductive heart. And it earns its place in the "I need to be released" category. On that note, let's get started…

Find Your "I'm Releasing Judgment" Power Statement

You know we all do it! It's not just me. Find something that suits your personal brand of judgment—we all have our favorites. Do a Google search and find a starting point that might lead you out of your negative thinking. Clearly see your struggle, even your addiction to judgment, and put it on the chopping block. Let's say it's judging others by their clothes, makeup, lack of makeup, car, home, color, hair, not to mention judgment about an ex-spouse or partner, or anyone you've struggled with! There's just so much opportunity!

Get specific with the judgment you're holding in your mind, notice how our judgment can also be a free for all, an all encompassing personality trait that sometimes affects all your interactions and communication. And when you can see it clearly, when you have examples of your judgment in your sight, just go for the judgment jugular vein. Hit it with your Power Statement. *No one above, no one below. There are no human enemies, there are only people in pain, asking for help.*

Here's where you want to do your research. Find a Power Statement or concept that will do battle for you, something you can thrive in. It's a word, phrase, or idea that helps you take charge of judgment and helps you replace it with a new concept that rejuvenates the heart and works as an antidote to negate this habit of the mind. It helps you think differently, to see the world through a new lens. And don't forget, when you find it, take note.

Mirror Neurons

Mirror neurons are nerves that get activated within a person when they observe an action performed by someone else. This neurological activation mirrors the biology of whatever the observer is watching—mirroring it within as though they were preforming the action themselves. The end result is that the observer creates a neurological body memory just by watching an activity, and it establishes a certain brain-body familiarity with the action being observed. It's an example of learning by example, at the level of our neurology. These kinds of neurons have been directly observed in many animals, but particularly in primate species.

Mirror neurons may also have the ability to be activated and reinforced through thought, activated through our internal observations and immigration. Through the act of playing a tape in your mind or imagining the ability to participate in a particular way in life, we can reinforce neurological patterning that helps us build internal frameworks for our life. It's creative thought, stimulating life first through your thinking and creating reflections within that help you build a supporting neurology that helps create a desired way of being. It requires the belief that the possibility exists to pattern yourself in new, strong, healthy, and good ways.

ROSCOE

True story: I used to tell a girlfriend I was exercising because I was thinking about it. Visualizing it. I figured I was activating my mirror neurons and getting buff! She never did buy it. I figured it was worth a try. But what it did do was create a neurology where I had a strong desire to stay physical and fit. I'm in pretty good shape, although I could be a bit more buff!

So get creative! Activate all your wonderful, very personalized mirror neurons. Get the bio-human in you moving forward, creating, and exploring life! Neurologically expand into your Power Statements, read books, listen to talks and podcasts, and *Look, Feel, Become* your best you. There are all kinds of social media to help, movies, YouTube, Google searches, Instagram, all have tools and messages to be found that can help you journey toward your truth. Explore all your words, their meanings and their strength. Spend your hours searching out quotes that speak to you. Explore what sparks you, music, prayers of the masters, ancient cultures, let them all unfold through you. And let the world and your imagination influence your heart-centered journey.

In Conclusion
Lastly, Finally, to Sum It Up...
(There's no end, just plenty more beginnings!)

Power Statements are about finding and exploring the components of life, and the ways of being that keep you moving in this world through your heart. My hope is that the Power Statements you choose allow their gift, their lesson, and the depth of their purpose to continuously move you. That their truths unfold in all the best of ways within you, and provide their wisdom, now and in your future.

Your Power Statements help guide your inner world so that you never have to question whether your heart has played its role well. They impact the quality of your experience and profoundly influence your world for the better when your intention is held with the integrity of your truth.

ROSCOE

I hope all your choices in life can be made through a unity between your heart and mind, because we come to the world with choices that have to move through us, choices that require the attention of the mind and heart. And it's in this unity, this cooperation of heart and mind, that all true choice evolves. This is the framework that all choices are designed to function through, and it's through that fusion that we find our freedom to choose well.

Mediated through the heart, there are no right or wrong choices, and it becomes impossible to choose wrong. Difficult choices with difficult consequences, yes. Sad, perhaps, but wrong when moving through the honesty and integrity of the heart? No. With heart and mind united in understanding, every choice comes with its gift; it comes presenting a lesson, and a purpose deeper than itself. They won't always feel perfect and right, but moving through the heart, we know the feeling of that choice, and we'll know it was the best we could choose in that moment of our lives. There's a grace in that, an almost automatic self-forgiveness we can unfold into when we know we've done our best in the moment.

So allow yourself to be guided by your wise and precious heart. Allow for heart-centered guidance, and find ways to remember and hold what wisdom you've invited forward.

It's up to you to do your work in this human experiment, and when you do, the whole world benefits from your courage.

So welcome to your journey, welcome to your life.

ABOUT THE AUTHOR

Brian Roscoe

DR. ROSCOE specializes in multiple forms of holistic techniques that teach the clients the power behind releasing the emotions that limit life. Through his work on integrating the body, mind, and spirit, Dr. Roscoe helps patients form a deeper understanding of their ability to heal their internal world. He helps them explore some of the many levels of personal growth, while engaging their journey with more meaning, discovering their unique internal wisdom, and restoring a life based in self-love.

DrBrianRoscoe.com
BrianRoscoeAuthor.com

CONTINUE THE JOURNEY

books by Brian

Inspirational Espresso

Get your daily shot of inspiration! In his book, Inspirational Espresso, Dr. Brian Roscoe walks us through the importance of looking inward and questioning ourselves in the interest of cultivating a higher state of wellbeing and, therefore, a richer life experience. With little shots of wisdom guiding you to question your motives, integrity, and direction, Brian helps pave the way for choosing to learn to love better while maintaining a sense of compassion, understanding, and truth towards yourself and all others.

"Our purpose here in this wildly marvelous world is to remember how to expand into a place of deep, multilayered, unconditional love – a love that is, in essence, who we already are and have always been."

Inspirational Espresso will leave hints of truth, inspire moments of wisdom and understanding, as well as mindfully helping us live our lives pointed toward a gentler, more compassionate way while immersed in this fantastic journey of living.

Call of the Heart: Six Secrets to Self-Love

CALL OF THE HEART is the gateway to your journey back to yourself. Roscoe presents a journey guided by love and self-discovery that will change your perspective on life, forgiveness, relationships, and your journey's purpose.

In this book, you will find:

- guidance and inspiration for living through love
- how to discover your inner worth and light
- how to see the gifts in your wounds
- introspective prompts to carry you along the journey
- Listen to the call of your heart, and journey through this book to uncover the six secrets to self-love.

Call of the Heart, Awakened: The Journey of Self-Love

CALL OF THE HEART, in its second installment, takes readers deeply into the journey of self-love. Using all of the insights and tools of the first Call of the Heart book, Awakened steps into the minds and aspirations of everyone who explores its pages, helping them see an enlightened way—the truth within themselves.

In this book, you will find:

- a deep dive into what it means to live with self-love
- how to manifest your inner gifts
- how to elevate your perspective
- introspective prompts to carry you along the journey
- Listen to the call of your heart, and journey more deeply into the remembering of your spirited self.

Power Statement Logbook: Mentoring the Habits of the Heart

THE POWER STATEMENT LOGBOOK is a companion guide to the Call of the Heart series. This workbook empowers readers to take charge of their journey by guiding them through meditations and musings on how to find, harness, and employ your personal power every single day.

In this book, you will find:

- deeper insights into the journey of self-love
- prompts to help stir your inner wanderer
- activities for introspection and growth
- guidance and tips for your journey ahead
- Listen to the call of your heart, and journey more deeply into your personal power.

The New-Now: The Art of Being Right Here, Right Now

We're here to activate a higher consciousness from within to reclaim our own miracle. Our journey was designed to be an inspired one, one we're all meant to embrace, and it's expressed through the gift of a world that infinitely unfolds into each unique life. So welcome. Welcome to your life. Welcome to the journey.

Are you ready to fully engage mindfulness?
Are you ready to honor each and every moment?
Are you ready for a new perspective?

Welcome to the New-Now.

PLEASE LEAVE A REVIEW

Public reviews help independent authors bring you the books you love. If you loved this book, please leave a review on Amazon. You can also leave your feedback on social media by connecting with Brian @drbrianroscoe. Thank you! And enjoy your journey!

www.ingramcontent.com/pod-product-compliance
Lightning Source LLC
Chambersburg PA
CBHW030438010526
44118CB00011B/699